Collins ATLAS
LONDON

Contents

Published by Collins
An imprint of HarperCollins Publishers
77-85 Fulham Palace Road, Hammersmith, London W6 8JB

Collins® is a registered trademark of HarperCollins Publishers Limited
Copyright © HarperCollins Publishers Ltd 2007
www.collins.co.uk

Mapping generated from Collins Bartholomew digital databases

Text on pages 3-57 researched and written by Karen Lloyd
Photographs on pages 39, 40, 48, 50, 52, 55 and 57 are courtesy of Visit London
Photograph on page 47 courtesy of Richard Knight

Printed in China   ISBN 978 0 00 725668 6
              Imp 001   VN12338   CDDL

e-mail: roadcheck@harpercollins.co.uk

2

London guide

Symbols used in the text

♧   Disabled facilities available. This does not necessarily mean that facilities are not available elsewhere. Always check before travelling.

⏰   London is full of fascinating things for children to see and do. This guide suggests just some of them with this symbol.

■   Buying a London Pass can be a cost effective way of seeing many of the capital's sights. For more details see page 7.

This symbol gives an indication of some of London's best known attractions. They are places not to miss on your trip to London.

Grid references (e.g. **77 D3**) are provided for all places shown on the mapping. All other places can be located using the street address, unless otherwise stated.

Essential information

Emergencies

The freephone numbers to use if someone is in immediate danger, or a crime is happening, are **999** or **112**. You will speak to an operator who will ask you if you need the police, ambulance or fire brigade. Keep calm, answer their questions carefully and help will soon be with you.

Accidents & ill health

◆ Hospitals

Holiday visitors, EU citizens and people from countries with reciprocal arrangements can receive free medical treatment at National Health Service (NHS) hospitals. Non-EU citizens can have free emergency treatment only in the Accident and Emergency (A&E) departments of NHS hospitals; if you need to be admitted to a ward, you will be charged. You will also be charged for any other treatment unless you have medical insurance. The following central London hospitals have A&E departments:

St. Mary's, Praed Street, W2	70 A2	☎ 020 7886 6666
St. Thomas', Lambeth Palace Road, SE1	84 B3	☎ 020 7188 7188
University College, Euston Road, NW1	64 B3	☎ 0845 155 5000

◆ Emergency dentists

Patients registered with a local dentist should contact their dental surgery for emergency treatment or answer machine information on out of hours arrangements. Visitors or residents not registered should telephone the 24 hour NHS Direct helpline (☎ 0845 4647) to find an emergency dentist in the area.

◆ Doctors & chemists

If you have a minor illness or ailment, either telephone the 24 hour NHS Direct helpline (☎ 0845 4647), or go to any chemists' shop (pharmacy/drugstore) where the pharmacist will be able to help you. The local police station will have a list of doctors in the area and if you need medication after normal closing time (5pm to 6pm), they will also have a list of late night chemists. In central London this will include:

Bliss chemists, 5-6 Marble Arch, W1	☎ 020 7723 6116
Boots chemists, Piccadilly Circus, W1	☎ 020 7734 6126
Boots chemists, 114 Queensway, W2	☎ 020 7229 1183
Zafash Pharmacy (open 24 hours), 233-235 Old Brompton Road, SW5	☎ 020 7373 2798

Car breakdown

If you are not already a member you can join some breakdown organisations at the roadside. There may be a surcharge for these services, so check when telephoning. The following telephone numbers are for use in the event of a breakdown:

Automobile Association (AA) ☎ 0800 887766
Green Flag ☎ 0800 051 0636
More Than ☎ 0800 300988
Royal Automobile Association (RAC) ☎ 0800 828282

Recovery services are also available from some local garages. Always ask for prices.

Lost property

Lost property found in the street is usually taken to the nearest police station so apply there. For property lost in other locations:

Black Cab, underground or bus.
The Lost Property Office, 200 Baker Street, NW1.
Allow 24 hours before enquiring. The office is open 8.30am to 4pm Mon to Fri. Personal identification is required and a charge is made on collection. ☎ 0845 330 9882

Docklands Light Railway.
DLR, Security Hut, Poplar Station. ☎ 020 7363 9550

Gatwick Airport.
Excess Baggage Company, South Terminal. Open Mon-Fri 8am to 5.30pm. A charge will be made on collection. ☎ 01293 503162

Heathrow Airport.
Information desk in relevant terminal ☎ 0870 0000 123. After 24 hours, airport Lost Property Office. Open Mon-Fri 8am to 5.30pm. A charge will be made on collection. ☎ 020 8745 7727

Railway stations.

Cannon Street	☎ 0845 000 2222	London Bridge	☎ 020 7234 1247
Charing Cross	☎ 020 7930 5444	Paddington	☎ 020 7313 1514
Euston	☎ 020 7387 8699	St Pancras Int	☎ 08457 221 125
King's Cross	☎ 020 7278 3310	Victoria	☎ 020 7963 0957
Liverpool Street	☎ 020 7247 4297	Waterloo	☎ 020 7401 7861

River services.
The boat operator, the pier office. ☎ 020 7941 2400

Stansted Airport.
Operated by OCS. Open 9.30am to 4.30pm daily. Items held for three months. Rising charge depending on how long it takes you to collect. ☎ 01279 663 293

Victoria Coach Station.
Victoria Coach Station, Help Point. 8am to 8pm every day. A charge is
made on collection. ☎ 020 7730 3466

If all else fails, contact The Lost Property Office at 200 Baker Street,
NW1. Most things left on public transport arrive there sooner or later!

◆ Lost or stolen credit cards

Immediately report lost or stolen credit cards to the issuing company,
using their emergency phone numbers:

American Express ☎ 01273 696 933	**NatWest** ☎ 0870 600 0459
Barclaycard ☎ 0870 154 0154	**Royal Bank of**
HSBC ☎ 0845 600 7010	**Scotland** ☎ 0126 829 8929
Lloyds TSB ☎ 0800 096 9779	**Visa** ☎ 0800 89 1725
Mastercard ☎ 0800 96 4767	

Money

◆ Currency

The pound sterling (£) is divided into 100 pence (p). Coin values are 1p,
2p, 5p, 10p, 20p, 50p, £1 and £2. Notes are £5, £10, £20 and £50.

◆ Banks

Most banks are open on weekdays from 9.30am to 5pm, and have at
least one ATM (cash dispensing machine). Many main branches are also
open for a shorter period on Saturdays. One branch of each of the four
major banks is listed below.

Barclays, 2 Victoria Street, Victoria, SW1 ☎ 08457 555 555
HSBC, 89 Buckingham Palace Road, SW1 ☎ 08457 404 404
Lloyds TSB, 179 Earls Court Road, SW5 ☎ 0845 300 0033
NatWest, 185 Sloane Street, Knightsbridge, SW1 ☎ 0845 303 0940

◆ Foreign exchange

The best rates of exchange are usually found in banks. However, Bureau
de Change are often open outside banking hours.
The Money Corporation,
18 Piccadilly, W1 ☎ 020 7439 2100
Thomas Exchange Global,
141 Victoria Street, SW1 ☎ 020 7828 1880
TTT Foreign Exchange Corporation,
The Plaza, 120 Oxford Street, W1 ☎ 020 7255 2555

◆ The Euro

Although the UK has not adopted the Euro, many large stores and services will accept it in their larger branches. Look for a sign on the door or ask a member of staff. At London airports, you can use Euro with NCP car parks and you can pay for train tickets in Euro on the Gatwick Express, Virgin Trains and the Stansted Express.

◆ Tax refunds on goods

If you are from a non-EU country, you can reclaim some of the tax you have paid on some of your shopping. For further information and to claim refunds try www.premiertaxfree.com or www.globalrefund.com

Passports & embassies

◆ Passports

As soon as you can, get a photocopy of the essential parts of your passport, particularly the number. This may speed things up if it needs to be replaced. If you do lose it or it is stolen, inform the local police immediately and contact your embassy or consulate.

◆ Embassies

The London Tourist Board website www.visitlondon.com has a list of all the major embassies in London, some of which are listed below. A London Black Cab taxi driver will always be able to take you to your embassy, even if you do not know the address.

Australia, Australia House, Strand WC2	☎ 020 7379 4334
France, 58 Knightsbridge, SW1X	☎ 020 7073 1000
Germany, 23 Belgrave Square, SW1	☎ 020 7824 1300
Japan, 101-104 Piccadilly, W1	☎ 020 7465 6500
South Africa, Trafalgar Square, WC2	☎ 020 7451 7299
United Arab Emirates, 30 Prince's Gate, SW7	☎ 020 7581 1281
USA, 5 Upper Grosvenor Street, W1	☎ 020 7499 9000

Public toilets

Look out for street signs saying 'toilets' or 'public toilets'. Bear in mind that many are locked after dark, except for the 24 hour unisex ones that look like shiny metal cabins; you need exactly the right coins to use these. All other public toilets are separated into male and female and there is sometimes a charge to use them. You will also find them in most public transport stations, except for the underground.

Visitors with disabilities

Some buses, trains and stations have facilities for disabled access, but not all, so it is advisable to check in advance before travelling on public transport. Contact Transport for London ☎ 020 7222 1234. Their free booklet *'Access to the Underground'* is available from www.tfl.gov.uk and also from Transport for London information centres. General information and advice is also available from the following organisations:

Artsline (arts and entertainment access), 54 Charlton Street, NW1
www.artsline.org.uk ☎ 020 7388 2227
DIAL (information and advice line)
www.dialuk.info ☎ 01302 310123
Disability Now, 6 Market Road, N7
www.disabilitynow.org.uk ☎ 020 7619 7323

For information on access to theatres www.theatre-access.co.uk
For information on access to restaurants www.viewlondon.co.uk
For information on access to pubs www.pubs.com

For manual and powered wheelchair hire, contact the Disabled Living Foundation www.dlf.org.uk ☎ 020 7289 6111

Tourist information centres

These can provide you with information on accommodation, trips and tours, current events and so on. If they do not have the answer, they can usually find someone who does. Personal callers are welcome at:
Britain Visitor Centre, 1 Regent Street, Piccadilly Circus, SW1 83 C1
London Visitor Centre, Waterloo International Terminal 85 C2
Southwark Tourist Information Centre, Tate Modern, SE1 85 D1
Alternatively, phone the Visit London information line
☎ 0870 156 6366

The London Pass

For good value on public transport and to beat queues at over 50 attractions, buy a 'London Pass'. You will also get discounts at some theatres and restaurants. You can buy a pass with or without transport, for 1,2,3 or 6 consecutive days. For example:

Without transport for **6** consecutive days	Adult £79.00	Child £55.00
With transport for **6** consecutive days	Adult £117.00	Child £75.00

Attractions shown with a 🎫 in this guide are covered by the pass, either for free entrance or discounts. Buy with a credit or debit card ☎ 0870 242 9988, or from any Exchange International, or on-line at www.londonpass.com

When to visit

The following list includes not only the most important annual events but also some of the more obscure and interesting London customs. For exact days, times and places contact Visit London ☎ 0870 156 6366

Annual events

New Year's Day Parade, 1st January.
A huge parade through the West End. All sorts of entertainment including American style marching bands, vintage cars and floats. Free. Parliament Square, through Trafalgar Square, Piccadilly Circus finishing on Piccadilly.
www.londonparade.co.uk   ☎ 020 8566 8586

London International Boat Show, January.
Built over the water, this exhibition venue has floating as well as static displays. Cost on application.
ExCeL, Royal Victoria Dock, E16   ☎ 0870 060 0246
www.londonboatshow.com

Chinese New Year, February.
Traditional Chinese celebrations. Free. Around Leicester Square, WC2

The London Marathon, April.
26 mile (42km) race through the streets of London. Spectators free.
Greenwich/Blackheath to The Mall

London Harness Horse Parade, Easter Monday.
Parade of horse drawn vehicles. Free. Battersea Park, SW11

Chelsea Flower Show, May, over five days.
The garden event of the year. Tickets can only be bought in advance. Full sized display gardens, plant companies from all over the world, wonderful scents in the floral pavilion. Plants can be purchased on the last day. Cost on application. No under 5s.
Royal Hospital, Chelsea, SW3   ☎ 020 7649 1885
www.rhs.org.uk

Beating Retreat, June, two evenings, 7pm to 8pm.
Cavalry, Guards and the Corps of Drums play spine tingling military music and drill as the sun sets. Tickets are priced from £10 and need to be booked in advance.
Horse Guards Parade, SW1   ☎ 020 7414 2271

Doggett's Coat and Badge Race, July.
The oldest annual sporting event in Britain dating from 1721. Five young men from the Watermen's Company row along the Thames in a race to win Doggett's Coat and Badge. Free.
London Bridge to Cadogan Pier, Chelsea Embankment
☎ 020 7361 2826

Royal Academy Summer Exhibition, June to August.
Works by painters, printmakers and sculptors at this contemporary art exhibition, the largest of its kind in the world. Some pieces are for sale. Cost on application.
Royal Academy, Burlington House, Piccadilly, W1   ☎ 020 7300 8000
www.royalacademy.org.uk

The Queen's Birthday Parade (Trooping the Colour), June.
Although Her Majesty's real birthday is on 21st April, she has an official birthday in June when the weather is, hopefully, better. This is a spectacular show of pageantry, when troops from the Household Division (foot and mounted) are inspected by the Queen who is also in uniform. After the bands have played some stirring music the regimental colour is passed down the ranks; originally, the flags were paraded past the troops so they would recognise them in battle. Finally, the Queen rides back to Buckingham Palace at the head of her Guards. Free but tickets need to be applied for well in advance.
Horse Guards Parade, SW1

The Proms, July to September.
The Henry Wood Promenade Concerts, a tradition since 1895. Quality classical music for all at low prices. Over 70 performances and always a good atmosphere. Book early. Cost on application.
Royal Albert Hall, Kensington Gore, SW7   ☎ 020 7589 8212

Notting Hill Carnival, August Bank Holiday.
A taste of the Caribbean in one of the world's largest street parties. Free.
Around W11 area

Fireworks Night, around 5th November.
A unique British celebration to commemorate the Gunpowder Plot, when the Houses of Parliament were nearly blown up around 400 years ago. Effigies of the plotters are burnt on a bonfire and fireworks are let off. Cost varies, some free.
Events all over London

London to Brighton Veteran Car Run, first Sunday in November.
A race for cars of pre-1905 vintage. The event celebrates the abolition of the law that required a man with a red flag to walk in front of all cars! Superb old vehicles from all over the world. Free.
Hyde Park (7.30am) to Brighton   ☎ 01327 856024

State opening of Parliament, October or November.
Although you cannot enter the Houses of Parliament, it is a wonderful opportunity to see the Queen and Duke of Edinburgh travel from Buckingham Palace in the magnificent gold State Coach. Free.
Houses of Parliament, SW1

Lord Mayor's Show, second Saturday in November.
The origins of this parade date from 1215, when the newly elected Mayor of London travelled to the Royal Courts of Justice to pledge allegiance to the Crown. The procession still takes place but now includes bands, floats and other entertainment. Money is collected en route for a charity selected by the Lord Mayor. The grand finale is a firework display over the Thames. Free.
Mansion House to the Royal Courts of Justice, Strand, WC2
www.lordmayorsshow.org   ☎ 020 7606 3030

Christmas lights, from the end of November.
Festive illuminations along with beautiful seasonal displays in the windows of all the large department stores; don't miss Hamley's Toy Shop. Free.
Oxford Street, Regent Street and Bond Street, W1

Christmas carols, late December
Westminster Abbey, SW1   ☎ 020 7222 5152
www.westminster-abbey.org

Daily events

◆ Changing of the Guard

Buckingham Palace 11.30am to 12.15pm either every day or alternate days. Cancelled in very wet weather.
The correct name for this ceremony is 'Guard Mounting'. A band accompanies the New Guard as they exchange duties with the Old Guard. The Queen's Guard is usually, but not always, the Foot Guards in the famous red and black uniforms with bearskin hats.
Watch from outside the palace railings. Free. 82 B2

Horse Guards Parade, 11am Mon to Sat, 10am Sun. Dismount ceremony daily at 4pm.
The Queen's Life Guard ride on splendid horses from Hyde Park Barracks at 10.28am Mon to Sat and 9.28am Sun. They pass Hyde Park Corner, Constitution Hill and The Mall, arriving at Horse Guards Arch where the ceremony takes place.
Whitehall, SW1   83 C1

Tower of London, 11.30am.
A small ceremony with fifteen men, one officer and five non-commissioned officers.
Tower Hill, EC3   77 D3

St. James's Palace, 10.45am to 11am.
Part of the Old Guard marches from St. James's Palace to Buckingham Palace, SW1   82 B1

◆ The Ceremony of the Keys

Tower of London, nightly at 9.53pm.
The ceremony of locking the Tower for the night has been carried out for the last 700 years. The Chief Warder walks from the Byward Tower carrying a candle lantern and the Queen's Keys. Various gates are locked en route, with all guards and sentries saluting the Keys. When they return to the Bloody Tower, the sentry there calls out a challenge, once satisfied that these are the Queen's Keys, the Chief Warder is allowed to proceed up the steps and calls *God preserve Queen Elizabeth*, the officer in charge replies *Amen*. The clock chimes ten and the Last Post is played. Tickets for the ceremony need to be applied for in advance.
Tower Hill, EC3   77 D3

◆ Speakers' Corner

Marble Arch, any time of day.
A remaining vestige of the British tradition of free speech is this institution of impromptu discourses by various speakers, usually on politics or religion. Free.
Marble Arch, corner of Hyde Park, W2   71 C3

Getting around

From airports to the city

London City Airport ☎ **020 7646 0088**
Two DLR services from the London City Airport Station linking to the
London Underground at Bank and Canning Town.

London Gatwick Airport ☎ **0870 000 2468**
Rail departure from south terminal to Victoria (non stop)
www.gatwickexpress.com ☎ 0845 850 1530. Alternatively there is a
Thameslink train to London Bridge, Blackfriars and King's Cross or a
coach connection to central London www.nationalexpress.com

London Heathrow Airport ☎ **0870 0000 123**
Underground connections at all terminals. There is also an express rail
service to Paddington ☎ 0845 600 1515 www.heathrowexpress.com
and a coach service to central London www.nationalexpress.com

London Stansted Airport ☎ **0870 0000 303**
Rail to Liverpool Street ☎ 0845 600 7245 www.stanstedexpress.com.
Coach connection to central London www.nationalexpress.com

Public transport

London has an extensive public transport network made up of rail,
underground, bus, light rail and riverboat services. To plan your journey
use the journey planner on www.tfl.gov.uk or phone the 24 hour travel
information line ☎ 020 7222 1234

◆ Buses

Bus stops in central London have roadside ticket machines from which a
ticket must be purchased before boarding a bus. There are two types of
bus stop, the white circle with white bar on a red background, where a
bus will always stop (unless it is full) and the same symbol with
REQUEST written on the white bar where a bus will only stop if you
hold out your arm to show the driver you want to be picked up. Each
stop has a destination list along with the number of the bus; this
information is repeated on the front of the bus. Ring the bell when you
want to get off. Discounts are available by use of an Oyster smartcard
(see p14). Under 16s travel free, but 14 and 15 year olds require a Child
Oyster photocard. Night buses run from 11pm to 6am from bus stop

signs with a dark blue background and yellow writing. The London Transport Travel Information Centre ☎ 020 7222 1234 will answer queries about timetables and fares and give journey planning advice.

◆ The Underground

The London Underground system, commonly known as the 'Tube', is the simplest way of getting around London and is a particularly efficient way to travel in the area of central London covered by this atlas. There are 12 colour coded lines and maps of the network are displayed in the stations and on the trains. Pre pay for journeys using the Oyster smartcard system, or buy a ticket at a ticket office or automatic machine at the station. There are six travel zones, and fares are linked to how many zones are travelled through. Tubes start running around 5.30am during the week and continue up to midnight. The Jubilee line has wheelchair accessible trains and stations can be accessed by lift. Most other stations have stairs or escalators, check the website for accessibility.

www.tfl.gov.uk   ☎ 020 7222 1234

◆ Rail

The Mainline stations in London are Paddington (serving the west), Euston, St. Pancras and King's Cross (north), Liverpool Street (east), Waterloo (south west) and London Bridge, Charing Cross and Victoria (south). Tickets can be bought from a travel agent or rail station and Travelcards can be used within the six London zones. All Eurostar trains, which run from St. Pancras International, are wheelchair accessible.
☎ 08457 48 49 50

◆ Coach

Victoria Coach Station in Buckingham Palace Road is the main coach station for National Express Coaches. Tickets can be purchased at the coach station (6am to 11.30pm daily), or ☎ 020 7730 3499.

◆ Docklands Light Railway (DLR) &

Built in 1987 to serve the Docklands area in East London, this system connects with the Underground system and runs from Bank to Beckton, with extensions to Lewisham, Stratford and London City Airport. The trains, in their red, white and blue livery are computer-controlled but do have a guard/ticket-collector on board. Travelcards are accepted. Wheelchair friendly.
www.tfl.gov.uk/dlr

Oyster, Travelcards & the London Pass

◆ Oyster

Oyster is London's smartcard system of travel payment. It can be used on card readers at underground and DLR stations, on buses and at tram stops. It allows pre-payment for travel which is cheaper than paying for single tickets. You can buy Oyster cards online at www.oystercard.com, at underground stations or from over 2000 appointed outlets across London. ☎ 0845 330 9876

◆ Travelcards

These are one day, 3 day, 7 day or monthly passes which allow unlimited travel on all public transport within particular zones. You can buy them at newsagents displaying a '*pass agent*' sign, or in rail and tube stations or in some Tourist Information Centres.

◆ DLR Rail & River Rover tickets

A ticket gives you one day's unlimited travel on City Cruises river boats and Docklands Light Railway ☎ 020 7363 9700 or www.dlr.co.uk

◆ The London Pass

Purchase of the London Pass gives free travel on buses, trains, Docklands Light Rail, Tramlink and the Underground. See the 'Essential information' section for details.

Taxis

The London 'Black Cabs' are not necessarily black any more, but if you want to travel in safety, with a driver who knows the streets of London thoroughly, use them. All these cabs have a yellow 'For Hire' sign, if it is lit up, they are free for hire. Hail one by waving, or you will find them at taxi ranks.

London Black Cabs &
Charges are by meter and are displayed in the cab. All have wheelchair ramps and other aids for the disabled. They run 24 hours a day, all year.
www.londonblackcabs.co.uk ☎ 07957 696673
Computer Cab ☎ 020 7908 0286
Dial a Cab ☎ 020 7251 0581
Radio Taxis ☎ 020 7272 0272

Car hire

Driving in London really is not much fun, especially in the rush hour. However, if you want a day out in the country, you could always hire a car. It is advisable to use a firm belonging to the British Vehicle Renting and Leasing Association (BVRLA) www.bvrla.co.uk.

Avis Rent a Car	☎ 0870 6060100
Europcar	☎ 0870 6075000
Hertz Rent a Car	☎ 0870 8415161
Sixt Kenning	☎ 0870 1567567

Different companies have different requirements, but for most you will need to be over 23 or 25; you will also require a driving licence. Check the car for damage before you leave and make sure this is documented. Finally, remember, drive on the left hand side of the road!

Driving around London

◆ Congestion charges

A charging zone encompasses the area of inner London. The £8 charge to enter this area applies only on weekdays between 7am and 6.30pm. Blue/orange badge holders from the EU are exempt provided they have registered and paid the one-off £10 charge. ☎ 0845 900 1234 or pay online at www.cclondon.com. Alternatively, pay at various outlets such as petrol stations and newsagents displaying the PayPoint logo.

◆ Parking

Parking spaces in London are few and expensive. The maximum stay is usually around two hours on a meter and most areas are restricted with double yellow (no parking at any time) or single yellow lines (no parking during working hours). You cannot park on a 'Red Route' at any time. Illegal parking can result in fines, wheel clamping or towing away. Privately run car parks (NCP ☎ 0870 606 7050 and **Masterpark** ☎ 0800 243 348 for example) are located all over the city.

Bicycle hire

Cycling in central London is not for the faint-hearted and not recommended for children. The roads are busy but the parks and quieter areas can be pleasant. You can just hire a bike or have a guided tour with a group.

The London Bicycle Tour Company 1a Gabriel's Wharf, SE1
www.londonbicycle.com ☎ 020 7928 6838
On Your Bike 52-54 Tooley Street, SE1
www.onyourbike.com ☎ 020 7378 6669

Places to stay

London offers a broad range of places to stay. The most expensive hotel accommodation is in the West End, with prices decreasing with distance from the centre. Self-catering could also be an option to consider. If you are on a tight budget, there are hostels, or even student Halls of Residence out of term time.

Booking accommodation

If you haven't already booked somewhere to stay, try the Visit London hotel booking service or an accommodation agency. There is usually a booking charge.

◆ Accommodation agencies & booking services

British Hotel Reservation Centre
Huge range. If you are not sure what you want, an advisor will help you.
www.bhrc.co.uk   ☎ 020 7592 3055

Hostels London
Online reservations for cheap hostel accommodation all over London.
Includes St. Christopher's Inns.
www.hostelslondon.net

International Booking Network (operated by Hostelling International)
Bed price varies with age (up to 18 and 18+).
www.hihostels.com   ☎ 01707 324170

London Bed & Breakfast Agency Ltd.
From £25 per person per night. Accommodation in private homes all over London.
71 Fellows Road, NW3
www.londonbb.com   ☎ 020 7586 2768

Visit London
A database of over 250 hotels in London including luxury accommodation, discounted rooms and last minute offers.
www.visitlondon.com   ☎ 08456 44 3010

Major hotels

Listed below are contact details for some of the larger hotel chains plus the more exclusive hotels. There is also a selection of accommodation at lower price ranges. Note that prices can vary depending on special deals, time of booking, booking agency deals etc.

The following symbols give a guide to price ranges:

£ = under £80/room	**£££** = £120 to £200
££ = £80 to £120	**££££** = £200+

◆ Selected hotels

Bedford
Pleasant hotel with 184 rooms. **From £**
Southampton Row, WC1   73 D1   ☎ 020 7636 7822

Bonnington Bloomsbury
A pleasant hotel with excellent facilities for disabled guests. **££**
92 Southampton Row, WC1   73 D1   ☎ 020 7242 2828

Claridge's
Patronised by the rich and famous, this is a very exclusive hotel,
203 rooms. **££££**
Brook Street, W1   72 A3   ☎ 020 7629 8860

Danubius
Modern 11 storey hotel, 376 rooms. Opposite Lord's Cricket Ground. **££**
18 Lodge Road, NW8   62 B2   ☎ 020 7722 7722

Dolphin Square
An all-suite hotel set in lovely gardens near the Thames. **£££**
Chichester Street, SW1   92 B2   ☎ 020 7834 3800

Dorchester
Overlooking Hyde Park, this stylish hotel has sumptuous rooms. **££££**
Park Lane, W1   81 D1   ☎ 020 7629 8888

Durrants
Comfortable, friendly and traditionally English. Near Oxford Street. **£££**
George Street, W1   71 D1   ☎ 020 7935 8131

Ibis
A modern 380 room hotel convenient for Euston. **£**
3 Cardington Street, NW1   64 B2   ☎ 020 7388 7777

Jurys, Islington
Modern hotel with 229 rooms. **From £**
60 Pentonville Road, N1   67 C1   ☎ 020 7282 5500

Mandeville
An Edwardian hotel with 166 rooms and modern facilities. **££££**
Mandeville Place, W1   71 D2   ☎ 020 7935 5599

Millennium Mayfair
A luxurious Georgian hotel overlooking Grosvenor Square. **From £**
Grosvenor Square, W1   71 D3   ☎ 020 7629 9400

Ritz
Luxury hotel with French elegance. All rooms are decorated in the Ritz colour schemes of blue, peach, pink and yellow. Traditional features and state of the art facilities. **££££**
150 Piccadilly, W1   82 B1   ☎ 020 7493 8181

Rocco Forte Brown's
The oldest hotel in London with a 'country house' atmosphere. Afternoon tea here is world famous. Unique, exclusive and luxurious, 117 rooms. **££££**
Albemarle Street, W1   72 B3   ☎ 020 7493 6020

Savoy
Luxurious hotel. Very Art Deco with 260 rooms, some overlooking the Thames. In the heart of West End theatre land. **££££**
Strand, WC2   74 B3   ☎ 020 7836 4343

Sherlock Holmes
Stunningly refurbished hotel with modern elegance and many luxurious facilities. **From ££**
108 Baker Street, W1   71 C1   ☎ 020 7486 6161

Sloane Square
An elegant 105 room hotel in fashionable Sloane Square. **££**
Sloane Square, SW1   91 D1   ☎ 020 7896 9988

Tavistock
Art Deco hotel overlooking the gardens of Tavistock Square. **From £**
Tavistock Square, WC1   65 C3   ☎ 020 7636 8383

Thistle Bloomsbury
A fine Edwardian hotel with 138 rooms. **From ££**
Bloomsbury Way, WC1   73 D1   ☎ 0870 333 9103

Thistle Bloomsbury Park
Comfortable hotel with 95 rooms. **££**
126 Southampton Row, WC1   73 D1   ☎ 0870 333 9104

Travelodge London Farringdon
Good hotel in central London with 211 rooms. **From £**
10-42 King's Cross Road, WC1   66 B2   ☎ 0870 191 1774

Waldorf Hilton
All 299 rooms in this distinctive luxury hotel are designed in an
Edwardian style. Impressive health and leisure suite. **££££**
Aldwych, WC2   74 B3   ☎ 020 7836 2400

Westminster
Close to Paddington rail station but in a quiet garden square. Modern,
comfortable and friendly. 116 rooms. **£ to £££**
16 Leinster Square, W2   68 B2   ☎ 020 7221 9131

◆ Hotel chains

Comfort Inns, Quality Hotels & Sleep Inn Hotels
Comfortable, good value hotels at convenient locations. **From £**
www.choicehotelseurope.com   ☎ 0800 44 44 44

Grange Hotels
New, luxury hotels all over central London with all the comforts you
would expect from top of the range accommodation. **From ££**
www.grangehotels.com   ☎ 020 7233 7888

Hilton Hotels
Top of the range luxury hotels. The Hilton Park Lane is the flagship of
the Hilton Group. Very modern, with 450 rooms on 28 storeys. **££££**
www.hilton.com   ☎ 08705 90 90 90

Holiday Inn Hotels
Mid-range comfortable hotels. **From ££**
www.ichotelsgroup.com   ☎ 0870 400 9670

Marriott Hotels
Comfortable hotels at convenient locations. **£££**
www.marriott.co.uk   ☎ 00800 1927 1927

Premier Inn Hotels
Good, basic hotels aiming to provide everything you need for a good
night's sleep. **£**
www.premierinn.com   ☎ 0870 242 8000

Thistle Hotel chain
Mid-price range hotels all over London. **From ££**
www.thistlehotels.com   ☎ 0870 414 1516

Eating & drinking

Restaurants

London is a haven for the gastronome, with food from every corner of the globe. Some restaurants are expensive, some are better than others and it is always wise to book. The list below does not include the excellent hotel restaurants, it is simply a very small selection from some of the better establishments dedicated to providing delicious cuisine. To book online, try www.visitlondon.com

◆ African

Pasha
Cosy, atmospheric restaurant, large choice of traditional food.
1 Gloucester Road, SW7 ☎ 020 7589 7969

Calabash
Next to Covent Garden, this reasonably priced restaurant offers excellent food with vegetarian options.
The Africa Centre, 38 King Street, WC2 ☎ 020 7836 1976

◆ American

Christopher's
Good pre-theatre menu with friendly staff and pleasant ambience.
18 Wellington Street, WC2 ☎ 020 7240 4222

Black & Blue
High quality, fresh, simple food cooked well, especially the beef. Friendly staff and good value for money. No booking.
215-217 Kensington Church Street, W8 ☎ 020 7727 0004

Hard Rock Café 🖱
Good food and service, rock music and great atmosphere. Queues to get in but you can pre-book.
150 Old Park Lane, W1 ☎ 020 7514 1700
www.hardrock.com

◆ Belgian

Belgo Centraal
Superb seafood, friendly staff, wide choice of Belgian beers.
50 Earlham Street, WC2 ☎ 020 7813 2233
www.belgo-restaurants.com

◆ British

Porters English Restaurant
Traditional, good value, English food and great atmosphere.
17 Henrietta Street, WC2 ☎ 020 7836 6466
www.porters.uk.com

The Oxo Tower Restaurant
Serves modern British food with lovely views over London.
Oxo Tower Wharf, Barge House Street, SE1 ☎ 020 7803 3888
www.harveynichols.com

Rules
The oldest restaurant in London (1798). Traditional British food.
35 Maiden Lane, WC2 ☎ 020 7836 5314
www.rules.co.uk

◆ Chinese

Fung Shing
One of the best. Interesting speciality dishes and exceptional service.
15 Lisle Street, WC2 (Chinatown) ☎ 020 7437 1539
www.fungshing.co.uk

Tiger Lil's
Choose your own ingredients and have them cooked in front of you.
270 Upper Street, N1 ☎ 020 7226 1118

Choys
Attentive staff in this welcoming restaurant. Good choice of food.
172 Kings Road, SW3 ☎ 020 7352 9085

◆ French

Le Café du Marche
First class service and food, extensive wine list. Quiet jazz downstairs.
22 Charterhouse Square, EC1 ☎ 020 7608 1609
www.cafedumarche.co.uk

Pied à Terre
High standards in food and service. Good value set menu for lunch.
34 Charlotte Street, W1 ☎ 020 7636 1178
www.pied-a-terre.co.uk

Mon Plaisir
Excellent French food at reasonable prices. Pre-theatre menu.
21 Monmouth Street, WC2 ☎ 020 7836 7243
www.monplaisir.co.uk

◆ Greek

Andreas
Delicious Greek food with a warm and friendly atmosphere.
22 Charlotte Street, W1   ☎ 020 7580 8971
www.andreas-restaurant.co.uk

The Real Greek
Tasty 'untypical' Greek food with friendly service. All the wine is Greek.
14-15 Hoxton Market, N1   ☎ 020 7739 8212
www.therealgreek.co.uk

◆ Hungarian

The Gay Hussar
Welcoming atmosphere and great Hungarian food.
2 Greek Street, W1   ☎ 020 7437 0973

◆ Indian

Rasa Samudra
Seafood from southern India, cooked well. Good vegetarian selection too.
5 Charlotte Street, W1   ☎ 020 7637 0222
www.rasarestaurants.com

Zaika
Excellent food recognised by the attainment of three AA rosettes.
1 Kensington High Street, W8   ☎ 020 7795 6533
www.zaika-restaurant.co.uk

Masala Zone
Authentic Indian food with outstanding, good value 'street food' dishes.
9 Marshall Street, W1   ☎ 020 7287 9966

◆ Irish

ArdRi at the O'Conor Don
Homely dining with friendly service and traditional food.
88 Marylebone Lane, W1   ☎ 020 7935 9311
www.oconordon.com

◆ Italian

Isolabella
High quality food and special service.
45-46 Red Lion Street, WC1   ☎ 020 7405 6830

Carluccio's Caffe Smithfield
Fresh, excellent food, wonderful ice cream. Very helpful staff.
12 West Smithfield, EC1 ☎ 020 7329 5904
www.carluccios.com

Sapori
Good Italian food, often with a unique twist. Friendly service.
43 Drury Lane, WC2 ☎ 020 7836 8296

Zafferano
Imaginative Italian food in this well established restaurant. Excellent
wine list.
15 Lowndes Street, SW1 ☎ 020 7235 5800
www.zafferanorestaurant.com

◆ Japanese

Benihana (Soho)
Entertaining chefs cooking excellent food.
37 Sackville Street, W1 ☎ 020 7494 2525
www.benihana.co.uk

Ginnan
Just excellent Japanese food. Good value lunchtime menu.
1 Rosebery Court, Rosebery Avenue, EC1 ☎ 020 7278 0008

◆ Korean

Han Kang
Good selection of fresh, well-prepared food.
16 Hanway Street, W1 ☎ 020 7637 1985

◆ Mexican

Café Pacifico
First rate margaritas along with a lively atmosphere and friendly service.
'Mexican Retro' decor representing all parts of Mexico.
5 Langley Street, WC2 ☎ 020 7379 7728
www.cafepacifico-laperla.com

◆ Middle East

Sofra (Covent Garden)
Appetising food, excellent service and reasonable prices. Seats 120 with
an additional 80 in the roof garden.
36 Tavistock Street, WC2 ☎ 020 7240 3773
www.sofra.co.uk

Maroush
Open until the early hours, good food and service.
38 Beauchamp Place, SW3 ☎ 020 7581 5434
www.maroush.com

◆ Scandinavian

Lundums
Classic Danish fayre cooked to perfection. Elegant but relaxed atmosphere.
119 Old Brompton Road, SW7 ☎ 020 7373 7774

◆ Spanish

La Rueda
Authentic Spanish food with dancing later.
102 Wigmore Street, W1 ☎ 020 7486 1718

La Tasca
Excellent food and helpful staff.
23-24 Maiden Lane, WC2 ☎ 020 7240 9062

◆ Thai

Nahm
Traditional Royal Thai cuisine in David Thompson's Michelin starred restaurant.
The Halkin, 5 Halkin Street, SW1 ☎ 020 7333 1234

Thai Terrace
Very good Thai food served in a friendly atmosphere.
14 Wrights Lane, W8 ☎ 020 7938 3585

Champor Champor (approximately translates to 'mix and match')
Small restaurant with excellent food and good service.
62 Weston Street, SE1 ☎ 020 7403 4600
www.champor-champor.com

◆ Vegetarian

Carnevale
A small mediterranean restaurant with a reasonably priced menu.
135 Whitecross Street, EC1Y ☎ 020 7250 3452

Food For Thought
Small cosy restaurant with excellent, good value food.
31 Neal Street, WC2 ☎ 020 7836 9072

Mildred's
Tasty food in generous portions. Caters for wheat and dairy allergies.
45 Lexington Street, W1 ☎ 020 7494 1634
www.mildreds.co.uk

Fast food

Fast food is available all over London. Chains include **KFC** (chicken), **Strada** (excellent pizza), **Wagamama** (Japanese) and **Prêt-à-Manger** (sandwiches). For coffee and a snack, try chains such as **Costa Coffee** and **Starbucks**. Good individual places include **Bar Italia** in Soho, which provides coffee and a snack at almost any time, **Sweetings** in Queen Victoria Street (very old company serving excellent fish). **Clark & Sons** are an eel and pie shop in Exmouth Market and **Arkansas Café** is an American BBQ near Liverpool Street underground.

☼ If you have children with you, there are some admirable quick bite chains. Try **Ed's Diners'** (retro with milkshakes and burgers), **Café Rouge** (adult dining with kids portions and activity packs). **The Rainforest Café** in Soho has waterfalls, animated creatures, mist and exotic food, or **Planet Hollywood** has lots of entertainment. **Belgo Centraal** in Covent Garden serves sausage and mash with other children's favourites and under 12s can eat free. In Bloomsbury, **China House** is a good place for oriental food with children's portions and entertainment for them in the afternoons.

Afternoon tea

The very English tradition of afternoon tea can still be enjoyed in many establishments. The following offer the 'crème de la crème' of this institution.

Claridge's Hotel
Very elegant and civilised. Tea, accompanied by music, served in the Foyer and the Reading Room. Booking recommended. Smart casual dress. From 3pm to 5.30pm, cost from around £35 per person.
Brook Street, W1   72 A3   ☎ 020 7409 6307
www.theclaridgeshotellondon.com

The Dorchester Hotel
Potted palms, sumptuous sofas and marble columns. Booking recommended. Smart casual dress. Afternoon tea (served 3pm to 6pm) costs around £35 per person.
Park Lane, W1   81 D1   ☎ 020 7629 8888
www.dorchesterhotel.com

The Ritz Hotel
Tea served in the Palm Court amid chandeliers and potted palms.
Booking essential six weeks in advance. Smart casual dress. From
11.30am to 7.30pm, cost around £40 per person.
150 Piccadilly, W1   82 B1   ☎ 020 7493 8181
www.theritzlondon.com

Rocco Forte Brown's
Like a country house, with a pianist and, in the colder months, a roaring
fire. Booking recommended. Smart casual dress. Weekdays 3pm to
5.45pm, weekends from 2.30pm, cost around £33 per person.
Albemarle Street, W1   72 B3   ☎ 020 7493 6020
www.brownshotel.com

Pubs & wine bars

◆ Wine bar or pub?

The alternative to the traditional English pub is a wine bar. Generally, it
will be part of a restaurant or bistro, perhaps with pavement tables,
and it will specialise in wines, light beers and lager. A pub has a totally
different ambience; open fires, quiet rooms in an old building, polished
brass and 'real ale' (made from a traditional recipe and hand-pulled
from barrels). The line between pubs and wine bars is becoming ever
more blurred, however, with the improvements in food being served in
pubs and heavier beers on tap in wine bars.
Opening hours vary but are generally 11am to 11pm and many London
pubs are closed on Sundays. Note that the age limit for buying or
consuming alcohol is 18 and you must be 14 or over to go in. Children
under 14 can be taken by an adult into a pub serving food.

◆ Wine bars

El Vino 30 New Bridge Street, EC4, **Eatons** 1 Minster Pavement, Mincing
Lane, EC3, **Cork and Bottle** Cranbourne Street, Leicester Square, WC2,
Crusting Pipe The Market, Covent Garden, WC2, **Tappit Hen** William IV
Street, Covent Garden, WC2, **Cicada** St. John Street, EC1, **Fluid**
Charterhouse Street, EC1.

◆ Pubs

There are basically two types, chain and individual pubs. The former
include the Slug & Lettuce and J.D. Weatherspoons (who serve good
food and guest ales at bargain prices), the latter include 'traditional'
old pubs and those in newer re-vamped premises, often with a 'theme'.

Try some of the following 'traditional' pubs:

Anchor
Riverside pub with plenty of seating ouside.
Bankside, SE1   ☎ 020 7407 1577

Black Friar
Art nouveau outside, Edwardian 'Arts & Crafts' inside with good beer.
174 Queen Victoria Street, EC4   ☎ 020 7236 5474

Bunch of Grapes
Victorian pub with finely engraved 'snob' screens which kept the well-to-do away from the 'riff-raff'.
207 Brompton Road, SW3   ☎ 020 7589 4944

Lamb & Flag
This wooden framed building (one of London's last) was built in 1623 and serves real ale.
33 Rose Street, WC2   ☎ 020 7497 9504

Salisbury
Beautiful Victorian traditional pub.
90 St. Martin's Lane, WC2   ☎ 020 7836 5863

Spread Eagle
Right in the heart of Camden, a traditional pub serving real ales.
141 Albert Street, NW1   ☎ 020 7267 1410

The George
An ancient coaching inn dating back to the 1540s with balconies overlooking the courtyard. Owned by the National Trust.
77 Borough High Street, SE1   ☎ 020 7407 2056

The Hope
Real ales and sausage 'n' mash lunches.
15 Tottenham Street, W1   ☎ 020 7637 0896

The Sherlock Holmes
Classic London pub, cosy with lots of Sherlock Holmes memorabilia.
10 Northumberland Avenue, WC2   ☎ 020 7930 2644

◆ Less traditional but also excellent:

Bunker Bar
A very successful microbrewery in a contemporary setting.
41 Earlham Street, WC2   ☎ 020 7240 0606

Mash
Space age décor with real ale brewed in its own microbrewery.
19-21 Great Portland Street, W1   ☎ 020 7637 5555

Shopping

Shopping areas & markets

The many diverse shopping areas in London each have their own character. To find what you want, it is essential to determine in which area you are most likely to find it.

◆ Shopping areas

New Bond Street, W1
Large, well-known exclusive designer fashion, plus antiques. **72 A2**

Old Bond Street, W1
Wall to wall jewellery shops including Tiffany's and Cartier. **72 B3**

Knightsbridge, SW1
Haute couture shopping and expensive, unique, designer *objets d'art* and antiques. **81 C2**

Oxford Street, W1 www.oxfordstreet.co.uk
Mainly leading high street department stores. **71 D2**

Regent Street, W1/SW1 www.regentstreetonline.com
More 'up market' department stores, smaller fashion shops, jewellery and china. Excellent for Christmas shopping when the illuminations are a sight in themselves. **72 B3**

Burlington Arcade, W1 www.burlington-arcade.co.uk
Famous, traditional London shops in a bygone setting. Uniformed guards make sure that shopping here is a calm and pleasant experience. **72 B3**

Carnaby Street, W1 www.carnaby.co.uk
Funky fashion, contemporary designer jewellery and anything trendy. **72 B2**

Charing Cross Road, WC2
Book shops galore. Foyle's (the biggest) down to small, specialist stores. **73 C2**

Denmark Street, WC2
A number of shops specialising in musical instruments. **73 C2**

Hatton Garden, EC1 www.hatton-garden.net
The place for jewellery. Over 60 glittering shops where you can buy or commission stunning pieces. **75 C1**

Jermyn Street, SW1 www.jermynstreet.net
Bespoke gentlemen's clothing. **82 B1**

Kings Road, SW3
Small, exclusive boutiques. 91 C1

Savile Row, W1
World famous for its bespoke tailors, you can purchase hand-made suits and superior 'off the peg' versions. 72 B3

St. James Street, SW1
Really interesting 'one off' shops selling hats, boots, cigars etc. 82 B1

Tottenham Court Road, W1
Bargain electrical goods, mainly computers and hi-fi. 64 B3

◆ Markets

There are hundreds of markets in London ranging from open-air craft markets to Sunday morning street markets selling clothes and general household goods. They can often be the place to seek out special items or unusual fashions.

Bermondsey Market
The largest antiques market in London. Fri from 4am.
Bermondsey Square, SE1   87 C3

Borough Market www.boroughmarket.org.uk
Gourmet food in abundance, from organic vegetables to hand-made cheeses and Morecambe Bay shrimps. Open from 11am on Thurs, noon on Fri and 9am on Sat.
Southwark Street, SE1   86 B1

Covent Garden Market www.coventgardenmarket.com
Wonderful original crafts. Open daily from 10am, 11am on Sun.
Covent Garden, WC2   73 D3

Grays Antique Market www.graysantiques.com
Over 80 dealers housed in one building. Open Mon to Fri from 10am.
58 Davies Street, W1   72 A3

Leadenhall Market www.leadenhallmarket.co.uk
Next to the amazing Lloyd's of London building designed by Richard Rogers, this food market sells traditional meats and fish along with specialist foods such as chocolate. Mon to Fri from 7am.
Whittington Avenue, EC3   77 C2

Old Spitalfields Market www.oldspitalfieldsmarket.com
With over 200 stalls on a Sunday, selling everything from organic food to jewellery, you can spend the day here. Open from 11am.
Commercial Street, E1   77 D1

Petticoat Lane
Open Mon to Fri from 10am, Sun 9am to 2pm. This market is famous for
clothes; be they genuine retro or last year's designer. Leather wear is a
speciality. Also bric-a-brac.
Middlesex Street, E1   77 D1

Other well known markets outside the area of this guide include
Camden Markets, NW1, **Columbia Road Flower Market**, E2 and
Portobello Road, W11.

The big stores

There are several large stores in London where you can buy practically
anything. Others are slightly more specialised, but still offer a wide
choice of goods.

Debenhams
Fashions and homeware at competitive prices, plus much more.
334-348 Oxford Street, W1   72 A2   ☎ 08445 616161
www.debenhams.com

Fenwick
Fashions for men and women on five floors. Also beauty products and a
beauty studio.
63 New Bond Street, W1   72 A3   ☎ 020 7629 9161
www.fenwick.co.uk

Fortnum & Mason
Almost 300 years old, this famous old store still sells the best in food;
teas, hampers and confectionery now sit alongside fine porcelain, linens
and other quality wares.
181 Piccadilly, W1   82 B1   ☎ 020 7734 8040
www.fortnumandmason.com

Hamleys
At 240 years old, this is still considered to be the best toyshop in the
world. Seven floors of toys, games and gifts. Toy demonstrations and
events going on all the time.
188-196 Regent Street, W1   72 B3   ☎ 0800 2802 444
www.hamleys.com

Harrods
Everything you would expect in a department store, plus a very famous
food hall and 26 restaurants!
87-135 Brompton Road, SW1   81 C3   ☎ 020 7730 1234
www.harrods.com

Harvey Nichols
Best known for its designer clothes, Harvey Nichols stocks some of the best of British, European, American and Far Eastern names.
109-125 Knightsbridge, SW1   81 C2   ☎ 020 7235 5000
www.harveynichols.com

John Lewis
Competitive pricing and a huge range of goods makes a visit to one of London's largest department stores well worthwhile.
Oxford Street, W1   72 A2   ☎ 020 7629 7711
www.johnlewis.com

Liberty
This purpose built store sells beautiful fabrics influenced by the Arts and Crafts movement. Clothes, bedlinens, furnishings and gifts.
210 Regent Street, W1   77 B2   ☎ 020 7734 1234
www.liberty.co.uk

Lillywhites
Everything you could want for every type of sport under one roof.
24-36 Regent Street, SW1   73 C3   ☎ 0870 3339600
www.lillywhites.co.uk

Marks & Spencer
This flagship store not only has a wide selection of clothes, homewares and food but it also has a bureau de change and instant cash refunds for tax-free eligible customers.
Marble Arch, W1   71 D2   ☎ 020 7935 7954
www2.marksandspencer.com

Selfridges
Six floors of everything, including fashion, household goods and a famous food hall and perfumery.
Oxford Street, W1   71 D2   ☎ 020 7318 2134
www.selfridges.co.uk

Specialist shops

London is an international centre for art, fashion, antiques and collectors' items. Many shops have specialised in certain goods and have become world-famous names. The list below represents only a selection of some of the best shops in each category.

◆ Antiques

Antiquarius Antique Centre, 131-141 Kings Road, SW3. Everything. Haggling acceptable.

David Aaron Ancient Arts, 22 Berkeley Square, W1. Antiques and rare carpets.
Kensington Church Street, W8. A mecca of internationally renowned antique shops. **78 A1-B2**
Map World, 25 Burlington Arcade, W1. Antique maps and atlases.

◆ Auctioneers

Bonham's, 101 New Bond Street, W1. Flagship London saleroom for fine art and antiques. **72 A2**
Christie's, 8 King Street, SW1. Fine art auctioneers since 1766. **82 B1**
Sotheby's, 34-35 New Bond Street, W1. World famous auction house for paintings, ceramics, glass, furniture, jewellery and books. **72 A3**

◆ Books

European Bookshop, 5 Warwick Street, W1. Wide selection of books and periodicals in many European languages.
Foyles 📷, 113-119 Charing Cross Road, WC2. The biggest independent bookshop.
Maggs Brothers, 50 Berkeley Square, W1. Antique and rare books.
Murder One, 76-78 Charing Cross Road, WC2. Books of 'orrible' murder stories, both real life and fiction.
Stanford's, 12-14 Long Acre, WC2. Books on travel and all the maps you could need.
Ulysses, 40 Museum Street, WC1. First editions from the 20th century.
Waterstones, 203-206 Piccadilly, W1. One of the largest general bookstores in London.

◆ China, glass & silver

London Silver Vaults, 53-64 Chancery Lane, WC2. Over 30 underground shops selling antique and modern silver. **75 C1**
Thomas Goode, South Audley Street, W1. Exclusive china, glass and silver.

◆ Clothes

Burberry, 157-167 Regent Street, W1. Famous trenchcoats plus lots more.
Jean-Paul Gaultier, 171-175 Draycott Avenue, SW3. Designer clothes.
Pringle, New Bond Street, W1. Luxury knitwear.
Rigby & Peller, 22 Conduit Street, W1. Lingerie made to measure.
Tracey Neuls, 29 Marylebone Lane, W1. Unique shoes.

◆ Jewellery

Angela Hale, 5 Royal Arcade, Bond Street. Art Deco and 50s style jewellery.
Asprey, 167 New Bond Street, W1. The Crown Jewellers, making and selling exquisite pieces.
Stephen Einhorn, 210 Upper Street, N1. Bespoke jewellery.
The Great Frog, 10 Ganton Street, W1. Gothic-style pieces.
Tiffany & Co., 25 Old Bond Street, W1. THE jewellers!

◆ Music

Hobgoblin, 24 Rathbone Place, W1. Traditional folk and Celtic musical instruments.
Rough Trade, 16 Neals Yard, WC2. Independent record store from which grew the now defunct record label of the same name.
Stern's, 74-75 Warren Street, W1. African music of all types.

◆ Perfume

Floris, 89 Jermyn Street, SW1. Classic Floris fragrances in a really beautiful shop.
Jo Malone, 150 Sloane Street, SW1. Fragrance combining, facials, hand and arm massage.

◆ One offs

Chocolat Chocolat, The Brunswick, Brunswick Square. Unique chocolates made on the premises.
Falkiner Fine Papers, 76 Southampton Row, WC1. Decorative and hand-made paper for wrapping or writing.
James Lock & Co, St. James Street, SW1. A wide range of hats for men and women.
James Smith & Sons, 53 New Oxford Street, W1. Umbrellas and walking sticks from the oldest shop of its kind in Europe!
Lulu Guinness, 3 Ellis Street, SW1. Unique handbags.
Paxton and Whitfield, 93 Jermyn Street, SW1. Cheeses, cheeses and more cheeses!
The Tea House, Covent Garden. Huge selection of teas and tea requisites.

Entertainment

London hosts world-class events and exhibitions. It also boasts a thriving night life. See the latest blockbuster at one of the many cinemas or a show at one of the famous West End theatres.

Booking tickets

Lists of current cinema, theatre, dance, music and comedy performances can be found in national newspapers, the *Evening Standard* newspaper and *Time Out* magazine. When booking, ask to see a seating plan (is the view restricted?), if necessary ask for details on disabled access and do not buy from people on the street.

◆ Box Offices

If you call in at a theatre and buy in person, there is usually no booking fee, if you book by telephone, there might be. The box office is usually open from 10am until just after the start of the performance. On the day, you may be fortunate and get a returned ticket or standby ticket.

◆ 'tkts' Ticket booth, Leicester Square

This is in the clocktower building and sells discounted tickets on the day of the performance. Seat positions cannot be specified. The Society of London Theatre's only official booth.

◆ Ticket agencies

The choice is vast, and most are genuine. Make sure they are members of an organisation called STAR. There is always a booking fee and sometimes a transaction fee. Find out the true price of the ticket from the theatre first, the booking fee should be no more than 25% of this. Some members of STAR are:

Ticketmaster ☎ 0870 154 4040 www.ticketmaster.co.uk
London Theatre Direct ☎ 0871 733 1001 www.londontheatredirect.com
or in person at Virgin Megastores in Oxford Street and Piccadilly Circus.

◆ Online

Buy online from the theatre website.

Cinemas

◆ Leicester Square cinemas showing the latest films

Many of the larger cinemas are centred on Leicester Square, WC2. They screen the latest releases and are the venues for glitzy film premieres.

Cineworld Shaftesbury Avenue	73 C3	☎ 0871 200 2000
Empire Leicester Square	73 C3	☎ 08714 714714
Odeon Leicester Square	73 C3	☎ 0871 2244007
Odeon West End	73 C3	☎ 0871 2244007
Vue West End	73 C3	☎ 08712 240240

◆ Other cinemas showing the latest films

Cineworld Fulham Road		
142 Fulham Road, SW10	89 C2	☎ 0871 200 2000
Cineworld Haymarket 63-65 Haymarket, SW1	73 C3	☎ 0871 200 2000
Curzon Mayfair 38 Curzon Street, W1	82 A1	☎ 0871 7033 989
Odeon Covent Garden		
135 Shaftesbury Avenue, WC2	73 C2	☎ 0871 2244007
Odeon Marble Arch 10 Edgware Road, W2	71 C2	☎ 0871 2244007
Odeon Panton Street		
11-18 Panton Street, SW1	73 C3	☎ 0871 2244007
Odeon Tottenham Court Road		
Tottenham Court Road, W1	73 C1	☎ 0870 5050007
Odeon Whiteleys Queensway, W2	68 B2	☎ 0871 2244007

◆ Independents

Barbican
Latest films, independent and arthouse.
Silk Street, EC2 76 A1 ☎ 020 7638 8891

BFI London IMAX
The UK's biggest cinema screen. 2D and 3D films.
1 Charlie Chaplin Walk, SE1 85 C1 ☎ 0870 7872 525

Ciné Lumière
French, European and world films with English subtitles.
17 Queensberry Place, SW7 90 A1 ☎ 020 7073 1350

Curzon, Soho
Mostly arthouse and independent films.
Shaftesbury Avenue, W1 73 C3 ☎ 0871 7033 988

National Film Theatre
Three screens showing everything from blockbusters to old classics.
Belvedere Road, South Bank, SE1 84 B1 ☎ 020 7928 3232

Prince Charles
Classic, recent and cult films. Also Sing-a-long nights.
Leicester Place, WC2 73 C3 ☎ 0870 8112 559

Theatres

The tradition of live theatre in London has flourished for more than four centuries. Today a wide range of productions are available, offering something for everyone. Various offers with the 'London Pass'.

◆ Theatres with backstage tours

Barbican ♿ www.barbican.org.uk
Purpose-built for the Royal Shakespeare Company. The theatre has a main auditorium for large scale productions and there is the Pit, a smaller studio for new works.
Silk Street, EC2   76 A1   ☎ 0845 120 7500
                                       ☎ 020 7628 3351 (backstage tours)

Duke of York ♿ www.theambassadors.com
Peter Pan first appeared here! Smaller theatre showing West End plays.
St. Martin's Lane, WC2   73 D3   ☎ 0870 060 6623
                                       ☎ 020 7836 4615 (backstage tours)

London Palladium ♿ www.rutheatres.com
Large theatre, famous for variety shows.
Argyll Street, W1   72 B2   ☎ 0870 830 0200
                                       ☎ 020 7850 8770 (backstage tours)

National Theatre ♿ 🅿 www.nationaltheatre.org.uk
Famous for its high standards, this repertory theatre has three auditoriums (the Olivier, Lyttelton and Cottesloe) which stage classics, new plays and musicals. Parking, restaurants, bookshop.
South Bank, SE1   85 C1   ☎ 020 7452 3000
                                       ☎ 020 7452 3400 (backstage tours)

Shakespeare's Globe 🅿 www.shakespeares-globe.org
Reconstruction of the original which was built nearby in 1599. No mod cons, as close as you can get to a 16th century performance. Also largest exhibition in the world about 'the Bard'.
21 New Globe Walk, Bankside, SE1   86 A1   ☎ 020 7902 1400
                                       ☎ 020 7902 1500 (backstage tours)

Theatre Royal, Drury Lane ♿ www.rutheatres.com
Destroyed by fire several times, the oldest playhouse in the world has survived to stage the best plays and musicals.
Catherine Street, WC2   74 B2   ☎ 0870 830 0200

Theatre Royal, Haymarket ♿ www.trh.co.uk
Grade I listed building showing excellent plays.
Haymarket, SW1   73 C3   ☎ 020 7930 8890

◆ Other mainstream theatres

Adelphi ♿ Strand, WC2	73 D3	☎	0870 264 3333
Aldwych ♿ Aldwych, WC2	74 B2	☎	020 7379 3367
Apollo Shaftesbury Avenue, W1	73 C3	☎	0870 154 4040
Apollo Victoria ♿ Wilton Road, SW1	82 B3	☎	0870 154 4040
Arts Great Newport Street, WC2	73 C3	☎	0844 847 1608
Criterion ♿ Piccadilly Circus, W1	73 C3	☎	0870 060 2313
Dominion ♿ Tottenham Court Road, W1	73 C2	☎	0870 154 4040
Duchess Catherine Street, WC2	74 B3	☎	0870 154 4040
Fortune Russell Street, WC2	73 D2	☎	0870 060 6626
Garrick ♿ Charing Cross Road, WC2	73 D3	☎	0870 040 0083
Gielgud ♿ Shaftesbury Avenue, W1	73 C3	☎	0870 950 0915
Her Majesty's ♿ Haymarket, SW1	83 C1	☎	0870 154 4040
Lyric ♿ Shaftesbury Avenue, W1	73 C3	☎	0870 154 4040
New London ♿ Drury Lane, WC2	73 D2	☎	0870 154 4040
Noël Coward ♿ St. Martin's Lane, WC2	73 D3	☎	0870 950 0920
Old Vic ♿ Waterloo Road, SE1	85 C2	☎	0870 060 6628
Palace ♿ Shaftesbury Avenue, W1	73 C2	☎	0870 890 0142
Phoenix ♿ Charing Cross Road, WC2	73 C2	☎	0870 060 6629
Piccadilly ♿ Denman Street, W1	73 C3	☎	0844 412 6666
Playhouse ♿ Northumberland Avenue, WC2	83 D1	☎	0870 060 6631
Prince Edward ♿ Old Compton Street, W1	73 C2	☎	0870 950 0915
Prince of Wales Coventry Street, W1	73 C3	☎	0870 950 0915
Queen's ♿ Shaftesbury Avenue, W1	73 C3	☎	0870 950 0915
Royal Court ♿ Sloane Square, SW1	91 D1	☎	020 7565 5000
St. Martin's ♿ West Street, WC2	73 D3	☎	020 7836 1443
Savoy ♿ Savoy Court, WC2	73 D3	☎	0870 164 8747
Shaftesbury ♿ Shaftesbury Avenue, W1	73 D2	☎	020 7379 5399
Trafalgar Studios 14 Whitehall, SW1	83 D1	☎	0870 060 6632
Vaudeville Strand, WC2	73 D3	☎	0870 890 0511
Victoria Palace ♿ Victoria Street, SW1	82 B3	☎	020 7834 1317
Wyndham's Charing Cross Road, WC2	73 C3	☎	0870 950 0915

Many Theatres use agency booking offices to give them more time to manage the theatre. Agency numbers have been given where this is the case.

◆ Fringe theatres

Bloomsbury 15 Gordon Street, WC1	65 C3	☎	020 7388 8822
Cochrane Southampton Row, WC1	74 B1	☎	020 7269 1606
Jermyn Street 16b Jermyn Street, SW1	72 B3	☎	020 7287 2875
Southwark Playhouse Shipwright Yard, SE1	86 A2	☎	0870 0601 761
Union 204 Union Street, SE1	85 D1	☎	020 7261 9876

◆ Open-air theatre

World-class performances from May/June to September in the beautiful setting of The Regent's Park, NW1. &
www.openairtheatre.org   **63 D2**   ☎ 08700 601811

Exhibition halls

Earls Court Exhibition Centre &
Hosts many large, high profile shows.
Old Brompton Road, SW5   **88 A2**   ☎ 020 7385 1200
www.eco.co.uk

Royal Horticultural Halls (Lawrence Hall & Lindley Hall) &
As well as hosting the famous flower shows, there are also antique fairs, wine tasting, record fairs and many other events.
80 Vincent Square, SW1   ☎ 0845 370 4606
Lawrence Hall, SW1   **83 C3**
Lindley Hall, SW1   **93 C1**
www.horticultural-halls.co.uk

Other major London exhibition centres outside the area of this guide:
ExCeL, Mace Gateway, E16
www.excel-london.co.uk   ☎ 020 7069 5000
Olympia, Hammersmith Road, W14 &
www.eco.co.uk   ☎ 020 7385 1200

Concert halls

Royal Festival Hall &
This modern hall, home of the London Philharmonic Orchestra hosts classical, jazz and contemporary music. The **Queen Elizabeth Hall** (chamber music, small orchestral works) and **Purcell Room** (chamber music and solo concerts) share the same site.
Belvedere Road, SE1   **84 B1**   ☎ 0871 663 2500
www.southbankcentre.co.uk

Royal Albert Hall &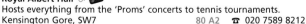
Hosts everything from the 'Proms' concerts to tennis tournaments.
Kensington Gore, SW7   **80 A2**   ☎ 020 7589 8212
www.royalalberthall.com

St. John's Concert Hall &
Classical music from symphony orchestras, choirs and solo performers.
Smith Square, SW1   **83 D3**   ☎ 020 7222 1061
www.sjss.org.uk

Wigmore Hall &
Major international artists and musicians making their London debut.
36 Wigmore Street, W1   72 A2   ☎ 020 7935 2141
www.wigmore-hall.org.uk

Opera & dance

Several venues in central London play host to leading national and
international ballet, dance and opera companies.

London Coliseum &
The home of the English National Opera, all performances are sung in
English. Ballet and contemporary dance share the venue. Backstage
tours available.
St. Martin's Lane, WC2   73 D3   ☎ 0870 145 0200
www.eno.org   ☎ 0870 145 2200 (backstage tours)

The Place &
Experimental and contemporary dance performances. Visitors welcome
and you can even have a go yourself!
17 Duke's Road, WC1
65 C2
☎ 020 7121 1100
www.theplace.org.uk

Royal Opera House &
Home to the Royal Ballet
and the Royal Opera.
Backstage tours available.
Covent Garden, WC2
73 D2
☎ 020 7304 4000
www.royalopera.org

Royal Opera House

Sadler's Wells &
The three theatres in this building stage international dance, opera and
musicals. Backstage tours available.
Rosebery Avenue, EC1   67 C2   ☎ 0844 412 4300
www.sadlers-wells.com

Places to visit

For general information on places to visit try www.visitlondon.com or phone the Visit London tourist information helpline ☎ 0870 156 6366. Always check 'last admission' time.

Royal London

Over hundreds of years, the British Royal Family has left its mark on the capital city. There are palaces, memorials, pageantry and shops by Royal Appointment. Many ceremonies can be seen throughout the year (see 'When to visit') and many buildings are open to the public.

Buckingham Palace

Banqueting House 🖼️   83 D1
The only surviving part of the Palace of Whitehall where Charles I was executed. Unique Rubens painting on the ceiling.
Mon to Sat 10am to 5pm.
Adults £4.50, with concessions.
Whitehall, SW1   ☎ 020 3166 6154
www.hrp.org.uk

Buckingham Palace State Rooms   82 A2
Built in 1705, this is the official London residence of the Queen. The 19 state rooms including the Throne Room, Ballroom and Picture Gallery and 42 acres of gardens are open to visitors during August and September. Treasures which can be seen include paintings by artists such as Rembrandt and superb examples of English and French furniture.
Open from 9.45am. Timed ticket system. Adult £15, with concessions.
St. James's Park, SW1   ☎ 020 7766 7300
www.royalcollection.org.uk   Disabled information ☎ 020 7766 7324

Kensington Palace 🖼️   78 B1
Home to the late Princess of Wales and other members of the Royal Family. The State Apartments, housing some of the Royal Collection and the Royal Ceremonial Dress Collection (which displays gowns dating from the 18th century) are open to the public.
Open daily from 10am. Adult £12 (Gate), with concessions.
Kensington Gardens, W8   ☎ 0844 482 7799
www.hrp.org.uk

The Queen's Gallery 🎫 ♿   82 A2
The gallery is part of Buckingham Palace and has a changing exhibition of priceless items from the Royal Collection.
Open most days from 10am. Adult £8, with concessions.
Timed ticket system.   ☎ 020 7766 7301
www.royalcollection.org.uk   Disabled information: ☎ 020 7766 7324

The Royal Mews 🎫 ♿   82 A3
A working stable with beautiful horses and a permanent display of State carriages and cars.
Open March to October, various times (sometimes closed for state visits). Adult £7, with concessions.   ☎ 020 7766 7302
www.royalcollection.org.uk

Tower of London ⏰ 🎫   77 D3
Dating from 1066, this wonderfully preserved medieval fortress has served many functions, from a residence for Royalty to a safe for the Crown Jewels. The collection includes the famous Koh-i-Noor diamond and the Imperial State Crown with its 317-carat diamond. The Yeomen Warders or Beefeaters give guided tours, dressed in their ancient livery, or you can explore the Tower independently.
Open March to October, Tue to Sat from 9am (Sun & Mon from 10am).
Winter Tue to Sat from 9am (Sun & Mon from 10am).
Adults £16, with concessions.
Tower Hill, EC3   ☎ 0844 482 7799
www.hrp.org.uk

Museums & galleries

London's national museums and galleries contain some of the richest collections in the world and are full of surprising treasures. They range from the vast British Museum to more recent and specialist additions, many of which incorporate interactive displays and exhibits. Many are free but there may be a charge for special exhibitions.

◆ Museums

British Museum ♿   73 D1
Founded in 1753, this is the oldest public museum in the world. It has almost 100 galleries, housing objects from all over the globe. The central courtyard has a modern glass and steel roof covering galleries, a reading room and a restaurant.
Opening hours vary for different areas. Phone for details. Guide and companion dogs welcome. Free.
Great Russell Street, WC1   Information line ☎ 020 7323 8299
www.britishmuseum.org   Box office ☎ 020 7323 8181

Bank of England Museum
76 B2

An interesting insight into the role of finance from the foundation of the bank in 1694. Besides displays of gold and banknotes, there are interactive exhibitions.
Open Mon to Fri. Free.
Threadneedle Street, EC2 ☎ 020 7601 5545
www.bankofengland.co.uk

Britain at War
87 C1

What life was really like for ordinary people in London during the Blitz of World War II. Sights, sounds and special effects recreate the terrifying atmosphere.
Open daily from 10am. Adult £9.95, with concessions.
64-66 Tooley Street, SE1 ☎ 020 7403 3171
www.britainatwar.co.uk

Clink Prison Museum
86 B1

Scenes showing the gruesome conditions in the prison.
Open daily from 10am. Adult £5, with concessions.
Soho Wharf, 1 Clink Street, SE1 ☎ 020 7403 0900
www.clink.co.uk

Design Museum
87 D2

Covering the last century of design, you can see everything from a Coke bottle to an Austin mini car. Also glimpses of futuristic prototypes.
Open daily from 10am. Adults £7, with concessions.
28 Shad Thames, SE1 ☎ 020 7940 8783
www.designmuseum.org

Golden Hinde
86 B1

A full size working reconstruction of Drake's 16th century galleon.
Open daily. Various workshops available. Self-guided tour, adults £3.50, with concessions. Guided tour (pre-booking required), adults £6, with concessions. Overnight stay available!
Clink Street, SE1 ☎ 0870 011 8700
www.goldenhinde.org

HMS Belfast
87 C1

World War II battleship on which you can explore all nine decks.
Open daily from 10am. Children under 16 must be accompanied by an adult. Adult £9.95, with concessions. Children under 16 free.
Morgan's Lane, Tooley Street, SE1 ☎ 020 7940 6300
www.hmsbelfast.iwm.org.uk

Imperial War Museum
85 C3

The national museum of war history. Open daily from 10am. Free.
Lambeth Road, SE1 ☎ 020 7416 5320
www.london.iwm.org.uk

London Dungeon ⏱   86 B1

Not recommended for the nervous or young children. This is a really scary experience with displays of horrific punishments and torture. The latest technology enables you to wander round the streets at the time of Jack the Ripper.
Open daily. Adults £19.95, with concessions.
28/34 Tooley Street, SE1   ☎ 0871 360 2049
www.thedungeons.com

London Transport Museum ⏱ ♿   73 D3

200 years of vehicles and memorabilia on display. Keep the children happy in 'KidZone', with its interactive exhibitions.
Open Sat to Thur from 10am, Fri from 11am.
Adults £8, under 16s free.
Covent Garden Piazza, WC2   ☎ 020 7379 6344
www.ltmuseum.co.uk

Madame Tussaud's ⏱ ♿   63 D3

Amazingly lifelike and life-size waxwork figures of villains and heroes from the past and present. Includes royalty, pop stars, film stars, statesmen and astronauts.
Open daily from 9am (9.30am off peak). Adults from £22.50 (online) prices vary according to date and time. Under 16s must be accompanied by an adult.
Marylebone Road, NW1   ☎ 0870 999 0046
www.madame-tussauds.com

Museum of London   76 A1

The fascinating story of London's social history, from prehistoric times to the present day, told through exhibitions and 'hands on' displays.
Open daily from 10am (12 noon Sunday). Free entry to most areas.
London Wall, EC2   ☎ 0870 444 3851
www.museumoflondon.org.uk   ☎ 0870 444 3850 (box office)

Natural History Museum ⏱ ♿   80 A3

Hundreds of excellent interactive exhibits covering all aspects of the natural world, from earthquakes to dinosaurs and the latest discoveries.
Open daily from 10am. Children under 12 must be accompanied by an adult. Free.
Cromwell Road, SW7   ☎ 020 7942 5011
www.nhm.ac.uk

Old Operating Theatre Museum 🔍   86 B1

The oldest surviving operating theatre in Britain, dating from 1822, restored to recreate the gruesome story of surgery before anaesthetics.
Open daily from 10.30am. Adults £5.25, with concessions.
9a St. Thomas Street, SE1   ☎ 020 7188 2679
www.thegarret.org.uk

Science Museum ⏰ ♿   80 A3
Seven floors housing stunning examples of the world's scientific inventions, covering everything from steam power to space exploration. Open daily from 10am. Free. Charges for IMAX, simulators and some special exhibitions.
Exhibition Road, SW7   ☎ 0870 870 4868
www.sciencemuseum.org.uk

The Bramah Museum of Tea and Coffee   86 A1
Everything you always wanted to know about these beverages, from the British perspective. From Trade wars and smuggling to ingenious coffee machines. Traditional tea room with full afternoon tea from £9. Shop selling a mouth-watering selection of teas and coffees.
Open daily from 10am to 6pm. Adults £4.
40 Southwark Street, SE1   ☎ 020 7403 5650 (information and table reservations)

Victoria & Albert Museum ⏰ ♿   80 A3
A superb museum of Decorative Arts, with jewellery, textiles, furniture and much more, some dating from 3000 BC. The last Friday of each month has a late night event.
Open daily, late on Wednesdays and the last Friday of each month. Free.
Cromwell Road, SW7   ☎ 020 7942 2000
www.vam.ac.uk   Advance booking for exhibitions ☎ 0870 906 3883

Vinopolis 📱 ♿   86 A1
Everything you could want to know about wine. Tours and wine tasting. Open daily from 12pm. Late on Mon, Thurs, Fri and Sat. Some exceptions, so phone first. Children allowed but no person under 18 allowed alcohol but fruit juice available. Adults £17.50 (self-guided wine tour), with concessions.
1 Bank End, SE1   ☎ 0870 241 4040
www.vinopolis.co.uk

◆ Galleries

Courtauld Institute of Art 📱 ♿   74 B3
Paintings, sculpture and other works of art, including Old Master, Impressionist and Post Impressionist paintings.
Open daily. Adults £5 with concessions, free for under 18s and Mon am.
Somerset House, Strand, WC2   ☎ 020 7872 0220
www.courtauld.ac.uk

National Gallery   73 C3
A 'must' for any art lover, this gallery houses Western European paintings from the mid-1200s to 1900, including Van Gogh, Rembrandt and Botticelli. Permanent and changing exhibitions.
Open daily from 10am, late on Wednesdays. Free.
Trafalgar Square, WC2   ☎ 020 7747 2885
www.nationalgallery.org.uk

National Portrait Gallery   73 C3

Likenesses of the famous and infamous, from the early 1600s painting of Shakespeare to modern icons from the sport and music worlds.
Open daily from 10am, late on Thur and Fri.
Free, except some special exhibitions.
St. Martin's Place, WC2   ☎ 020 7312 2463 (recorded)
www.npg.org.uk

Royal Academy of Arts   72 B3

A unique collection of mainly British art from the 1700s to the present.
Open daily from 10am, late on Fridays.
Charges vary for each exhibition.
Burlington House, Piccadilly, W1   ☎ 020 7300 8000
www.royalacademy.org.uk   Credit card booking ☎ 0870 8488 484

Saatchi Gallery   91 C2

Modern and sometimes controversial art, including works by Damien Hirst and Jenny Saville. The focus is to promote young British artists.
Open daily.
Sloane Square, SW1
www.saatchi-gallery.co.uk

Tate Britain   93 D1

The best of British art from 1500 to the present. See works by artists from Constable to Hockney, Gainsborough to Turner.
Open daily from 10am. Free, donations welcome.
Millbank, SW1   ☎ 020 7887 8888
www.tate.org.uk

Tate Modern   85 D1

Housed in the huge airy building that was the Bankside Power Station, are stunning masterpieces from 1900 to the present. Permanent and changing exhibitions feature Dali, Picasso and Warhol, as well as works by the latest contemporary artists.
Open daily from 10am, late on Fri and Sat.
Free, donations welcome.
Bankside, SE1   ☎ 020 7887 8888
www.tate.org.uk

Places of worship

Bevis Marks Synagogue   77 C2

Built in 1700, this is Britain's oldest surviving synagogue.
Open Sun to Wed and Fri from 11am to 1pm (10.30-12.30 Sun).
Bevis Marks, EC3   ☎ 020 7626 1274
www.bevismarks.org

London Central Mosque
62 B2

The centre for London's Muslims. Stunning 75ft (25m) high dome.
Telephone before visiting.
146 Park Road, NW8 ☎ 020 7724 3363
www.iccuk.org ☎ 020 7725 2212 (tours & visits)

St. Bartholomew-the-Great Church
75 D1

One of London's oldest churches, dating from the early 1100s.
Wonderful architecture and the setting for several films including
Shakespeare in Love and *Four Weddings and a Funeral*. Open Tue to
Sun from 8.30am (Sat from 10.30am). Tours available, phone first. Free.
Cloth Fair, EC1 ☎ 020 7606 5171
www.greatstbarts.com

St. Clement Danes Church
74 B2

Supposedly built by the Danes in the 9th century and rebuilt many times
since. Dedicated to the RAF in the 1950s. The nursery rhyme 'Oranges and
Lemons' probably refers to these bells. Free but donations welcome.
Strand, WC2 ☎ 020 7242 8282
www.st-clement-danes.co.uk

St. Mary-le-Bow church
76 A2

True Cockneys are born within the sound of the bells; Dick Whittington
is said to have heard them too. Golden dragon on the steeple. Free but
donations welcome. Open from 7am.
Cheapside, EC2 ☎ 020 7248 5139
www.stmarylebow.co.uk

St. Paul's Cathedral 📷 ♿
76 A2

This is probably Sir Christopher Wren's most famous building. Rising
from the ashes of the Great Fire of London, it was completed in 1710.
The magnificent dome affords superb views over London, as well as
containing the famous 'whispering gallery'.Open Mon to Sat from
8.30am. Services may close all or part of the building, phone first.
Adults £9.50, with concessions. Guided tours extra.
Ludgate Hill, EC4 ☎ 020 7246 8357
www.stpauls.co.uk ☎ 020 7246 8320 (wheelchair access)

Southwark Cathedral 📷 ♿
86 B1

The present cathedral dates from the early 1200s. The tower has a
superb view across the Thames, as shown in Hollar's famous drawing
'Long View of London'. A state of the art exhibition allows you to see
this view, along with many of the artefacts recently discovered.
Open Mon to Fri from 7.30am, Sat and Sun from 8.30am. Free but
minimum donation suggested £4 per person.
Borough High Street, SE1 ☎ 020 7367 6700
www.southwark.anglican.org

Westminster Abbey   83 D3

Housing the famous Coronation Chair, this building has seen the crowning of every new monarch (except two) since its foundation in 1065. The tomb of the Unknown Warrior resides here, representing all the fallen of World War I. Many poets are buried in 'Poets' Corner'. Open Mon to Sat from 9.30am. Special services may close all or part of the building, phone first. Cloisters open daily from 8am. Garden open Tue, Wed and Thur from 10am. Adults £10, with concessions. Garden, cloisters and services free. Free to wheelchair users.

Broad Sanctuary, SW1
☎ 020 7222 5152
www.westminster-abbey.org

Westminster Abbey

Westminster Cathedral   ♿   82 B3

This Cathedral is the headquarters of the Catholic Church in Britain. It is a Byzantine style building, built only a century ago and has the widest nave in England. Beautiful mosaics can be seen on the walls and floors. Free admission to church. Tower, Adults £5.

42 Francis Street, SW1   ☎ 020 7798 9055
www.westminstercathedral.org.uk

Monuments, statues & other landmarks

◆ Monuments & statues

Admiralty Arch, The Mall   83 C1
Unique memorial to Queen Victoria built in 1910, it has three identical arches with wrought iron gates.

Albert Memorial, Kensington Gardens   80 A2
Magnificent Gothic memorial to the husband of Queen Victoria. 175ft (53.3m) high, it holds a statue of Prince Albert who died in 1861. Tours 2pm and 3pm first Sun of each month Mar to Dec. Adults £4.50 plus concessions.   ☎ 020 7298 2000
www.royalparks.org.uk

Alfred the Great, Trinity Church Square   86 A3
Dating from the 14th century this is the oldest statue in London. It depicts one of the greatest Kings of England.

Big Ben (St. Stephen's Tower),
Parliament Square   83 D2
The famous four-faced clock (the
largest in Britain) sits in the 320ft
(106m) St. Stephen's Tower which
is part of the Houses of Parliament.
The name 'Big Ben' refers to the 14
tonne bell. Tours on request via your
MP only. No under 11s (UK residents)
Mon to Fri.
☎ 020 7219 4272
www.parliament.uk

Boadicea (Boudicca),
Victoria Embankment   83 D2
An imposing statue of the famous
British Queen and her daughters.
They are depicted in a chariot pulled
by galloping horses.

The Cenotaph, Whitehall   83 D2
The word means 'Empty tomb'.
The stark Portland stone column
commemorates those who died in the two World Wars.

Big Ben

Charles I, Trafalgar Square   83 D1
This is the oldest equestrian statue in London, dating from the 1600s.

Cleopatra's Needle, Victoria Embankment   74 B3
This 60ft (18m) high granite obelisk from Heliopolis dates from 1475 BC.
Erected in 1878, over a box and artefacts from that period.

Diana Memorial Playground, Kensington Gardens ♿   78 B1
Six different play areas, accessible to all children up to the age of 12.
Open daily 10am to dusk.   ☎ 020 7298 2141
www.royalparks.org.uk

Eros, Piccadilly Circus   73 C3
Representing the Angel of Christian Charity, this aluminium statue is a
memorial to Lord Shaftesbury.

London Peace Pagoda, Battersea Park   91 C3
The only pagoda in London, and the only monument in Britain
dedicated to world peace. Erected in 1985 by Japanese Buddhists.
www.batterseapark.org   ☎ 020 8871 7530

London Stone, Cannon Street   76 B3
Set into the wall of the Bank of China opposite Canon Street station
this piece of limestone is possibly a Roman milestone.

Marble Arch, north east corner of Hyde Park 71 C2
This white marble arch stands on the site of the notorious Tyburn Gallows, which for over 400 years saw public hangings. The arch was designed as an entrance for Buckingham Palace, but it was too narrow for the state coach to pass through so was moved to its present site.

The Monument, Monument Street 🚇 Closed until Dec 2008. 76 B3
This 202ft (61.5m) high portland stone pillar was designed by Sir Christopher Wren to commemorate the Great Fire of London. You can enjoy superb views by climbing up to the balcony via the 311 steps of the internal spiral staircase.
www.themonument.info ☎ 020 7626 2717

Nelson's Column, Trafalgar Square 83 C1
The 145ft (44m) granite column was raised in 1843. It is surmounted by a statue of Admiral Nelson, who died at the battle of Trafalgar after defeating Napoleon.

Peter Pan, Kensington Gardens 79 D1
This beautiful figure of the fictional character from J.M.Barrie's famous book was erected overnight in Kensington Gardens as a surprise for the children. The carved animals around the base have been partly worn away by children stroking them.
www.royalparks.org.uk

Queen Victoria Memorial, in front of Buckingham Palace 82 B2
A white marble sculpture of Queen Victoria, surrounded by various allegorical figures. At the top is a gilded figure of Victory.

Sir Winston Churchill, Parliament Square 83 D2
A powerful, modern bronze statue of one of Britain's great statesmen.

Wellington Arch, Hyde Park Corner 🚇 81 D2
Archway erected in 1828 with sculpture added in 1912. Viewing platform lift and exhibitions inside. Open Wed to Sun from 10am. Adult £3.20 plus concessions.
www.english-heritage.org.uk

Others to see
Achilles, Park Lane 81 D1. **Sir Charles Chaplin,** Leicester Square 73 D3. **Charles II,** Chelsea Hospital 91 D2. **Oliver Cromwell,** Old Palace Yard 83 D2. **Elizabeth I,** Fleet Street 75 C2. **Mahatma Gandhi,** Tavistock Square 65 C3. **Henry VIII,** St. Bartholomew's Hospital 75 D1. **Sir Thomas More,** Carey Street 74 B2. **Florence Nightingale,** Waterloo Place 83 C1. **Sir Walter Raleigh,** Whitehall 83 D1. **Richard the Lionheart,** Old Palace Yard 83 D3. **Captain Scott,** Waterloo Place 83 C1. **William Shakespeare,** Leicester Square 73 D3. **Duke of York,** Waterloo Place 83 C1.

◆ Bridges

Particularly noteworthy bridges across the Thames include:

Albert Bridge   90 B3
Unusual rigid chain suspension, built 1873.

Chelsea Bridge   92 A3
The original bridge was built in 1858 and was replaced by a suspension bridge in 1934.

London Bridge   86 B1
The original bridge was made of wood and built by the Romans. In the 12th century, it was replaced by a stone one, incorporating shops and houses which was famous for displaying the heads of traitors. The present bridge dates from 1973, the previous one having been sold to Lake Havasu City, Arizona.

Millennium Bridge   76 A3
London's newest bridge, with its 355 yard (325m) span, is a footbridge spanning the Thames from Bankside to St. Peter's Hill. It is a 'minimalist' stainless steel structure with a wooden walkway.

Tower Bridge

Tower Bridge   87 D1
The architecture of this well known Victorian-Gothic bridge was designed to complement that of the nearby Tower of London. Completed in 1894, it opens in the middle to allow tall ships through. This was made possible by hiding a steel frame inside the granite and Portland stone.

The London Bridge Exhibition 📷 provides a guided tour along the elevated pathways linking the two towers giving superb views of the city. The museum exhibition brings to life the human endeavour and engineering achievement which created this famous landmark. Open daily from 9.30am.
Adults £6, with concessions.   ☎ 020 7403 3761
www.towerbridge.org.uk

Waterloo Bridge   74 B3
Opened on the anniversary of the Battle of Waterloo, it was originally called Strand Bridge. It was replaced in 1942 by the present concrete structure designed by Sir Giles Gilbert Scott.

Westminster Bridge   84 B2
This graceful bridge is cast iron and was built in 1854.

Other central London bridges spanning the Thames include **Blackfriars** (1860) **75 D3**, **Lambeth** (1929) **94 A1** and **Southwark** (1921) **76 A3**.

◆ Plaques

Since 1867, blue plaques have been used to mark buildings in London where famous people have lived and worked. The oldest surviving ones date from 1875. To have a blue plaque, the person must have been dead for over 20 years and have made 'some important contribution to human welfare or happiness'. There are now over 800 official ones; many 'unofficial' plaques also exist. English Heritage ☎ 0870 333 1181

Libraries & other institutes

British Library &   65 C2
The national library of the UK welcomes visitors and has exhibition galleries, an events programme, a bookshop and tours of the building. Open daily from 9.30am (11am Sun). Reading rooms not open to the public without a reader's pass. Free entry to library and exhibitions. Tours, adults £8, with concessions. Phone for times.
96 Euston Road, NW1   ☎ 020 7412 7332 (visitor services)
www.bl.uk   ☎ 01937 546546 (box office)

Goethe-institut   80 A3
Events reflecting German culture. Plays, exhibitions, films and more.
50 Princes Gate, Exhibition Road, SW7   ☎ 020 7596 4000
www.geothe.de/ins/gb/lon/enindex.htm

Institut Français   90 A1
A centre for French culture. Cinema, library, talks and wine tastings.
Various opening times.
17 Queensbury Place, SW7   ☎ 020 7073 1350
www.institut-francais.org.uk

Parks & gardens

Since the second World War, there has been a concerted effort to increase the number of parks and green spaces in the city. There are some beautiful, tranquil retreats here, and the majority have free entry.

◆ The Royal Parks

These were originally the grounds of Royal Homes or Palaces and are still Crown property. They are open to the public and free to enter.
www.royalparks.org.uk

Green Park, The
82 A2

This park was once the meeting ground for duellists. The 47 acres (19ha) of grass, flower beds and trees are perfect for a picnic. Open daily.
☎ 020 7930 1793

Hyde Park

A Royal Park since 1536 and the most famous park in London. It contains a lake, the Serpentine, where you can hire a small craft or swim. Open daily 5am to midnight 80 B1 ☎ 020 7298 2100. You can wander and admire the various statues, or visit **Kensington Gardens**, the quiet end of Hyde Park, where you will find the Italian Fountain Gardens and memorials to the late Princess of Wales 78 B1.

Regent's Park, The
63 D2

Commissioned by Prince Albert, The Regent's Park has a host of attractions including London Zoo, a heronry and waterfowl collection and an open air theatre. Open daily, 5am to dusk   63 C1 ☎ 020 7486 7905. At the southern end are the beautifully laid out **Queen Mary's Gardens**.

The Regent's Park

St. James's Park
82 B2

Alongside The Mall, this is the oldest Royal Park. It boasts a beautiful lake with an island which is home to a colony of pelicans. There are excellent views of Whitehall and Buckingham Palace. On a summer's day you can hire a deckchair and listen to music at the bandstand. Open daily, 5am to midnight ☎ 020 7930 1793.

◆ Other parks & gardens

Camley Street Natural Park, Camley Street
65 C1

An interesting nature reserve, managed by the London Wildlife Trust.
www.wildlondon.org.uk
☎ 020 7833 2311

Chelsea Physic Garden, Royal Hospital Road
91 C3

Originally founded in 1673 to research the medicinal uses of plants; it also contains the oldest olive tree in Britain. Restricted opening, telephone first. Adults £7, with concessions.
☎ 020 7352 5646
www.chelseaphysicgarden.co.uk

Coram's Fields, 93 Guilford Street, WC1   66 B3
Seven acres of enjoyment for bored children. Complete with a pets corner, paddling pool, safe play equipment, café, large lawned areas and supervised activities. Disability friendly. Adults have to be accompanied by a child. Contact the office for forthcoming events.
www.coramsfields.org   ☎ 020 7837 6138

Finsbury Circus Garden, Finsbury Circus   76 B1
A public garden with the oldest pagoda tree in London, as well as plane trees dating from the mid 1800s.

St. Mary Aldermanbury's Garden, Aldermanbury   76 A2
A Victorian style knot garden incorporating the remains of Wren's church, medieval stonework and a bust of William Shakespeare.

Zoos & aquariums

London Aquarium ◎ 🔌 ♿   84 B2
Everything aquatic, from a freshwater stream to the Atlantic Ocean. Sharks, divers feeding conger eels and you can stroke the rayfish. Open daily from 10am. Prices vary according to time of year.
Adult £13.25, plus concessions.
County Hall, Westminster Bridge Road, SE1   ☎ 020 7967 8000
www.londonaquarium.co.uk

London Zoo ◎ 🔌 ♿   63 D1
With over 650 species, make sure you plan your visit so as not to miss a favourite daily event. London Zoo also has a conservation and breeding programme, helping to save some of the most endangered species on the planet and in the Millennium Conservation Centre, the 'Web of Life' explains the concept of biodiversity.
Open daily from 10am. Adult £14.50, with concessions.
Regent's Park, NW1   ☎ 020 7722 3333
www.zsl.org

Spectator sports

◆ Cricket

Lord's Cricket Ground   62 A2
Catch a test match, a one-day international or just a county game.
St. John's Wood, NW8   For a tour ☎ 020 7616 8595
www.lords.org   ☎ 020 7432 1000

The Oval Cricket Ground   94 B3
The home of Surrey County Cricket Club. The first test match in England was played here in 1880. Watch international cricket or a home game.
Kennington, SE11   ☎ 0871 2461 100
www.surreycricket.com

◆ Tennis

Wimbledon 📷
Outside the area of this guide, Wimbledon is probably the best known annual lawn tennis championship in the world.
www.wimbledon.org   ☎ 020 8944 1066

The Masters Tennis, Royal Albert Hall   80 A2
Top names playing in this December event.
Royal Albert Hall, SW7   ☎ 020 7070 4404 (box office)

◆ Athletics

London Marathon
In spring, over 30,000 serious and 'fun' runners take to the streets of London for this spectacular race.   ☎ 020 7902 0200
www.london-marathon.co.uk

Leisure activities

For **horse riding** in Hyde Park try:
Hyde Park Stables, 70 A3 ☎ 020 7723 2813
Ross Nye Stables, 70 A3 ☎ 020 7262 3791

For **ice skating**
Queens Ice Bowl 📷 , Bayswater, W2 68 B3 ☎ 020 7229 0172
Somerset House Ice Rink is a courtyard, which between the end of November and January, is transformed into a huge ice rink. In the evening it is floodlit. Lessons available. 74 B3 ☎ 0844 847 1520
Broadgate Ice Arena is an outdoor rink near Liverpool Street station. Open between October and April. 77 C1 ☎ 020 7505 4120

Sightseeing tours

◆ Guided walking tours

London Walks 📷
Guided walks with many different themes from a St. Patrick's Day pub walk to The Beatles Magical Mystery Tour. Walks last about two hours. First walk around 10am, last at 7.30pm. 7 days a week. £6. Children under 15 free (accompanied by parents) plus concessions.
www.walks.com   ☎ 020 7624 3978

Stepping Out
Specialising in smaller groups, guided walks include London City Ghost Walk, 2000 years of London history and Hidden London. A qualified London Guide is guaranteed. Short tours to all day so prices vary.
www.steppingoutlondon.co.uk   ☎ 020 8692 8411

And Did Those Feet....Guided Walks
These guided walks focus on the
archaeology and history of London,
with a bias towards the academic,
whilst still being entertaining.
249 Evering Road, E5
☎ 020 8806 4325
www.chr.org.uk

Personalised Walking Tours
Hire a 'Blue Badge' Guide;
reputedly the best.
£110 half day, £170 full day (more
for other languages).
57 Duke Street, Mayfair, W1
☎ 020 7495 5504
www.tourguides.co.uk

Jubilee Walkway

◆ Self-guided walking tours

Jubilee Walkway Self-guided 14 mile (23km) circular walk, with
information plaques sited at every junction. Leaflet from Visitor
Information centres www.jubileewalkway.org.uk
London Wall Walk A walk along part of the Roman City Wall, with
information panels.
Princess Diana Memorial Walk A seven mile (11km) walk through
several of the Royal Parks. Plaques mark the route. Wheelchair
accessible.

◆ Bus & coach tours

Original London Sightseeing Tour ☺
Hop on, hop off service operating from Victoria Coach Station.
Children's activities and a children's only channel of commentary. Daily.
Adult £19, Child £12.
Jews Road, Wandsworth, SW18   ☎ 020 8877 2120
www.theoriginaltour.com

Harrods Luxury Sightseeing
Luxury open topped buses introduce you to the sights. Book at Harrods.
Knightsbridge, SW1   ☎ 020 7225 6596

The Big Bus Company
The 24 hour hop on, hop off ticket includes a river cruise, discounted
entry to some attractions and three walking tours. Daily Adult £22,
Child £10.
35/37 Grosvenor Gardens, SW1
www.bigbus.co.uk   Info & credit card booking ☎ 020 7233 9533

Evan Evans
Operating since 1933. Pick up from over 60 hotels. Phone for prices.
258 Vauxhall Bridge Road, SW1 ☎ 020 7950 1777
www.evanevanstours.co.uk

◆ Car & taxi tours

London Taxi Tour
Ride in a London 'Black Cab'. Start from your hotel when you're ready.
7 Durweston Mews, W1 ☎ 07854 813576
www.blacktaxitours.com

Concierge Desk
A tour of London designed for you, with all entrance fees and tickets
organised. Book online. ☎ 020 8249 6055
www.conciergedesk.co.uk

◆ Bicycle

London Bicycle Tour Company
A cheap way to see London without getting stuck in traffic.
1a Gabriel's Wharf, 56 Upper Ground, SE1 ☎ 020 7928 6838
www.londonbicycle.com

◆ River & canal trips

London Duck Tours
Amphibious vehicles drive along the road then into the river on this 70
minute tour! Adult £19, Child £13, Concessions £15
55 York Road, SE1 ☎ 020 7928 3132
www.londonducktours.co.uk

City Cruises
Daily sailings from Westminster, Greenwich or Tower piers. Evening trips
in summer. Adults from £7.40 return.
www.citycruises.com ☎ 020 7740 0400

The London Waterbus Company
Canal boat trips on Regent's Canal from Camden Lock or Little Venice.
Summer 10am and hourly to 5pm. Winter (Sundays only) 10am and
hourly to 3pm. Return, adult £8.40, child £5.40. With inclusive London
Zoo ticket (one way) £16.50 adult and £13.50 child.
Camden Lock, NW1 and Little Venice, W2. ☎ 020 7482 2660
www.londonwaterbus.com

London from the air

Adventure Balloons
An original way of seeing London, with champagne thrown in! Take off sites all within a few miles of the Thames or the Tower of London.
www.adventureballoons.co.uk ☎ 01252 844222

Into the Blue
30 minute sightseeing flight by helicopter along the Thames. Flights go from Biggin Hill airport, Kent 17 miles (27km) south of the City.
30 minute tour £125.
www.intotheblue.co.uk ☎ 01959 578100

London Eye

London Eye ☺ ♿
On a clear day, you can see for 25 miles (40km) across London's famous landmarks from the world's largest observation wheel. Open daily from 9.30am. Adult £15, plus concessions.
Belvedere Road
☎ 0870 5000 600
(credit card booking)
☎ 0870 220 2223
(private capsule sales)
www.londoneye.com

Key to map pages

Primrose Hill

Kensal Rise

Kilburn

62 St. John's Wood

The Regent's Park

Maida Vale

68

70

MARYLEBONE

Notting Hill

BAYSWATER ROAD

PARK LANE

May

78

80

Hyde Park

KENSINGTON

Kensington Gardens

KNIGHTSBRIDGE

Belgravia

88

90

Brompton

CHELSEA

FULHAM RD

KING'S RD

Walham Green

FULHAM

Battersea Park

Scale

The maps on pages 62 to 95 are at a scale of 1:12,000 (approx 5¼ inches to 1 mile)

| 0 | 0.25 | 0.50 | 0.75 kilometre |

| 0 | ¼ | ½ mile |

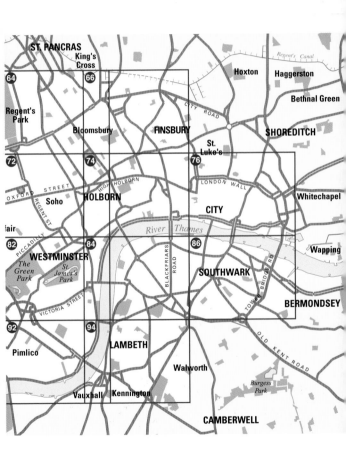

Key to map symbols

Public transport
Transports publics   Öffentliche Verkehrsmittel

Main railway station   **PADDINGTON**
Gare ferroviaire principale   Hauptbahnhof

Other railway station   VAUXHALL
Autre gare ferroviaire   Sonstiger Bahnhof

London Underground station   EDGWARE RD
Station de Métro Londonienne   Londoner U-Bahnhof

London Underground lines - colour code
Lignes de Métro de couleur   Farbkodierung der U-Bahnlinien

Bakerloo	East London	Metropolitan
Central	Hammersmith & City	Northern
Circle		Piccadilly
District	Jubilee	Victoria

Pedestrian ferry with landing stage   CADOGAN PIER
Bac à pied avec embarcadère   Fussfähre mit Landungssteg

Bus/Coach station   VICTORIA
Gare d'autobus et autocars   Bus-/Reisebus Haltestelle

Bus service terminal point
Terminal de la ligne d'autobus   Endstation der Buslinie

Regular daily service (bus routes & numbers)
Ligne quotidienne régulière   Regelmäßiger täglicher Dienst   2.36.185   88

One way bus route
Direction d'autobus   Einbahnstraße für Busverkehr   ←

Places of interest
Visites interessantes   Sehenswürdigkeiten

Building open to the public
Bâtiment ouvert au Public
Gebäude für die Öffentlichkeit zugänglich

Imperial War Museum

Other important building
Autre bâtiment important
Andere Sehenswerte Gebäude

Bank of England

Entertainment
Salles de spectacle   Unterhaltungsorte

Concert hall/Opera house
Salle de concert/Opéra   Konzertsaal/Oper   ROYAL OPERA HOUSE

Theatre   Théâtre   Theater   🎪 PALLADIUM

Cinema   Cinéma   Kino   🎬 ODEON

Shopping
Shopping   Einkaufsviertel

Principal shopping street
Principale rue commerçante   Haupteinkaufsstraße   NEW BOND ST

Shopping street
Rue commerçante   Geschäftstraße   Carnaby St

Major shop
Magasin important   Wichtiges Kaufhaus   Selfridges

Street market
Marché de rue   Straßenmarkt   ●

General information
Informations diverses   Allgemeine Informationen

Hospital   Hôpital   Krankenhaus   Guy's Hospital

Synagogue   Synagogue   Synagoge   ✡

Mosque   Mosquée   Moschee   ☾

Other place of worship
Autre lieu de culte   Andere Andachts/Kultstätte   +

Public toilet   Toilettes publiques   Öffentliche Toilette   🚻

Information centre for visitors
Syndicat d'Initiative   Touristeninformation   *i*

Major hotel   Grand hôtel   Wichtiges Hotel   Ritz

Public house   Pub   Kneipe   ★ Lamb & Flag PH

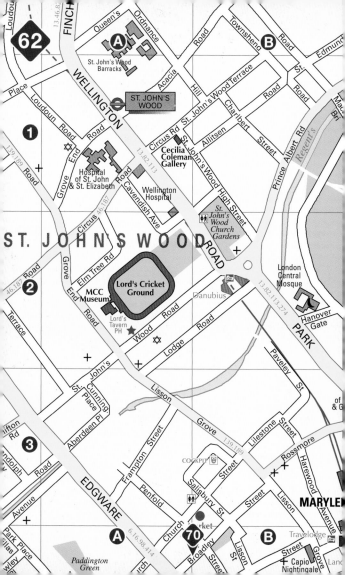

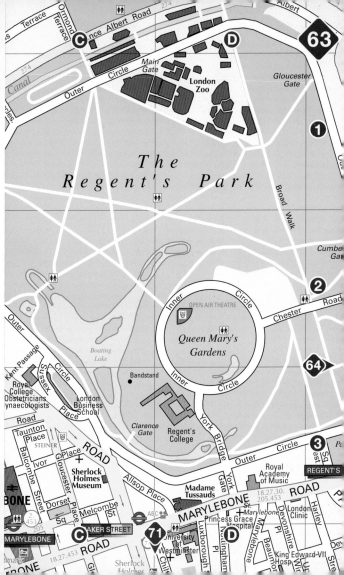

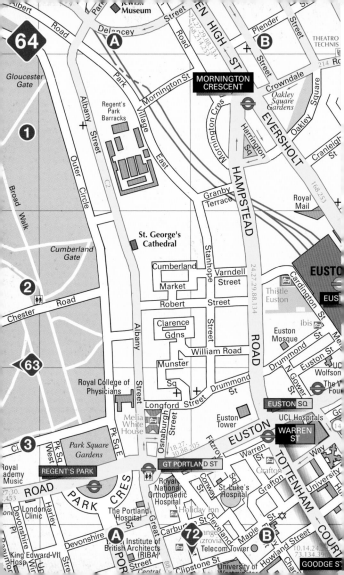

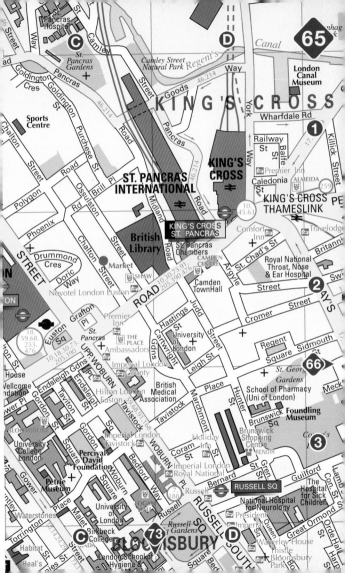

St. Pancras Hospital

St. Pancras Gardens

Camley Street Natural Park

Regent's

London Canal Museum

65

Canal

Camley St

Way

Goldington Cres

Goldington St

Pancras

Street

Goods Way

York Way

KING'S CROSS

Wharfdale Rd

1

Sports Centre

Chalton Street

Purchese St

Brill St

Road

Midland Road

ST. PANCRAS INTERNATIONAL

Railway St

Balfe St

Premier Inn

Caledonia St

ALMEIDA

259

KING'S CROSS

KING'S CROSS THAMESLINK

Polygon

Rd

Ossulston

Phoenix

St

Drummond Cres

Doric Way

STREET

British Library

British Library

Camden Street

KING'S CROSS ST. PANCRAS

10.45.63

St Pancras Chambers

CAMDEN CENTRE

St. Chad's St

Comfort Inn

Royal National Throat, Nose & Ear Hospital

Travelodge

Britanni

2

Novotel London Euston

Market

SHAW

10.30.73.91. 205.390.476

Camden Town Hall

Argyle

Street

St. Chad's

Street

St

ON

Euston Sq

18. 59.68. 253. 476

Grafton Pl

10.18.30.73 205.390

St. Pancras

Premier Inn

Ambassadors

Imperial London County

Hastings

Cartwright Gdns

University of London

Judd Street

Leigh St

Cromer

Regent Square

Street

Sidmouth

Street

St. George Gardens

Meck

66

House

Wellcome Foundation

Endsleigh Gdns

Gordon St

Endsleigh

Taviton St

Gordon

Square

Woburn

Place

IPL

Hilton London Euston

British Medical Association

Tavistock Square

Tavistock

Place

Marchmont

Hunter

School of Pharmacy (Uni of London)

Brunswick Square

Foundling Museum

3

BLOOMSBURY

University College London

Gower

Percival David Foundation

Petrie Museum

Woburn Square

Imperial London Tavistock

Bedford Way

Coram St

Imperial London Royal National

Bernard St

Holiday Inn

Brunswick Shopping Centre

RENOIR

Co's

RUSSELL SQ

The Hospital for Sick Children

Waterstones

Torrington

Malet Street

Birkbeck College

University of London

73

LOGAN HALL

188

RUSSELL SQ SOUTH

Russell Gardens

National Hospital for Neurology

President

Imperial

Guilford

Great Ormond

President

Waverley House Thistle Bloomsbury

Habitat

Heal's

London School of Hygiene &

C

D

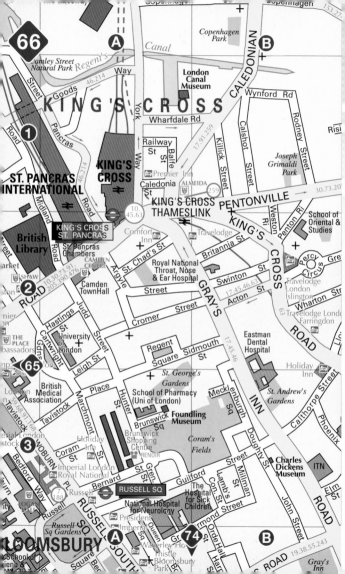

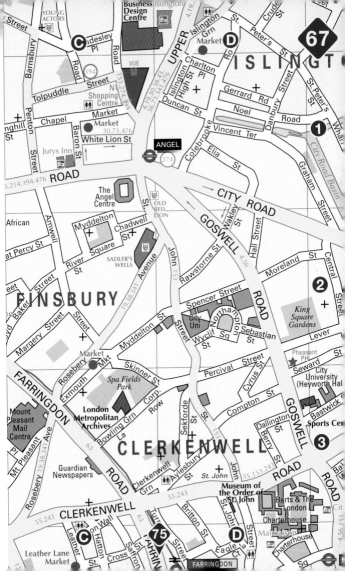

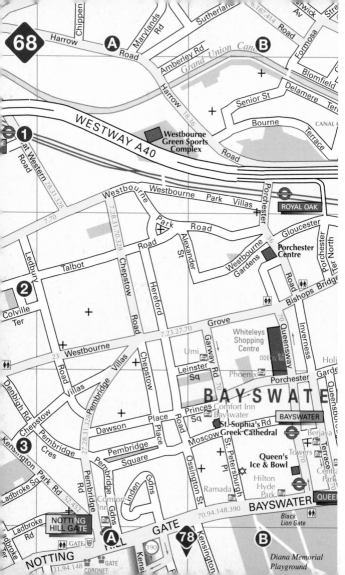

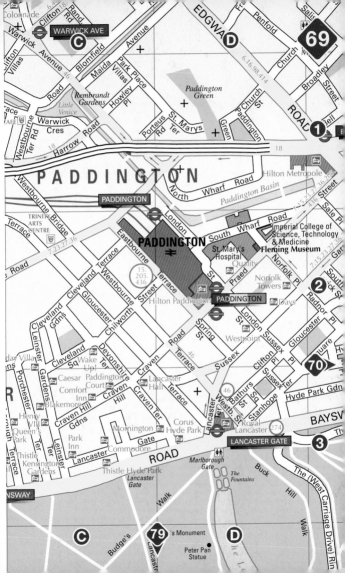

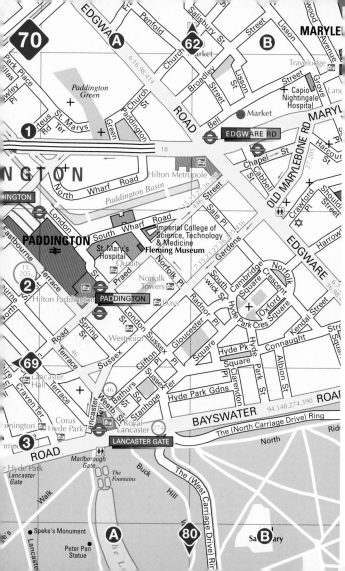

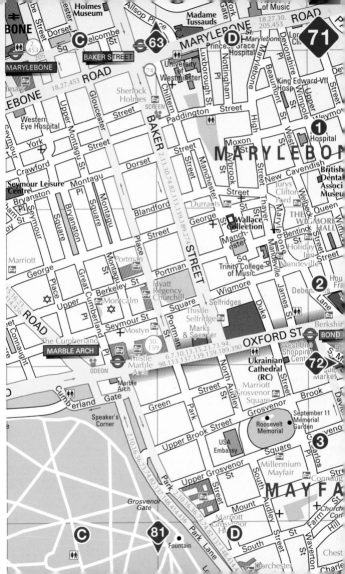

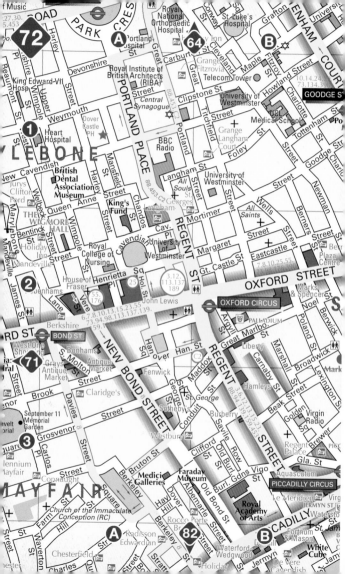

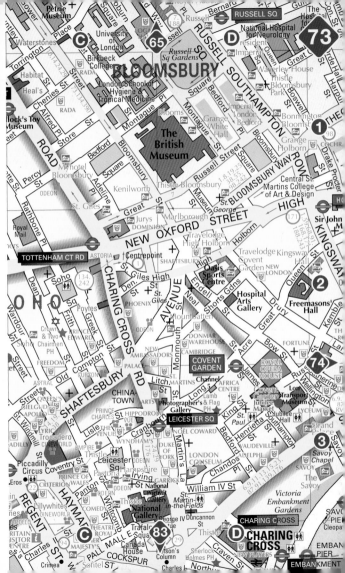

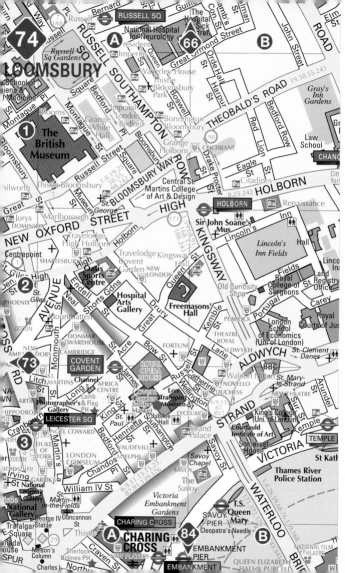

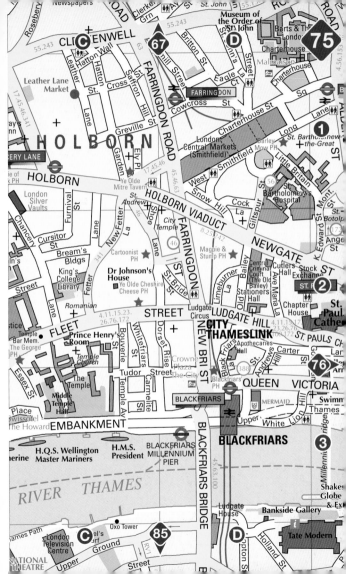

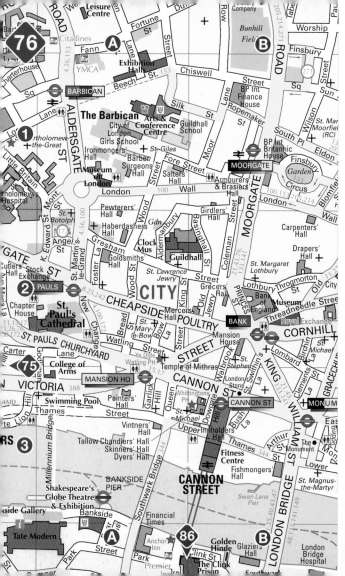

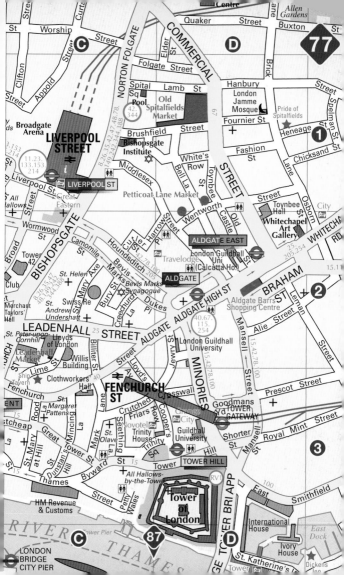

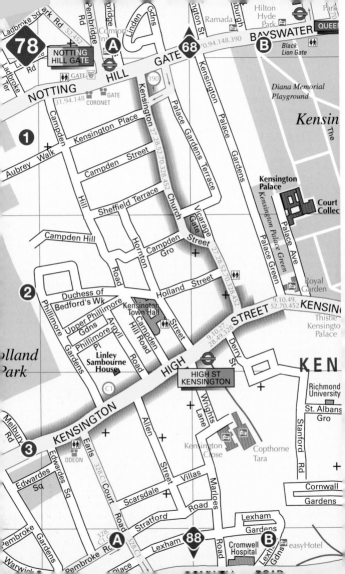

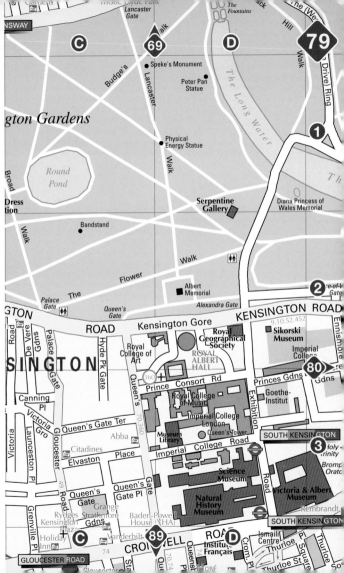

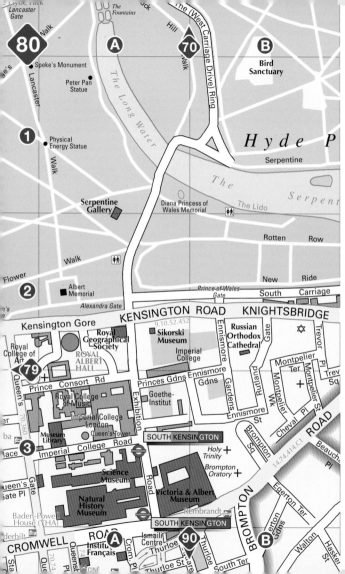

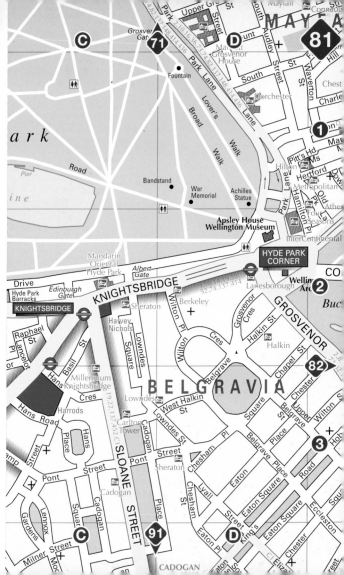

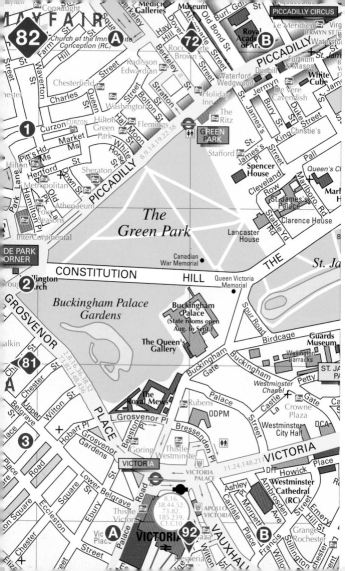

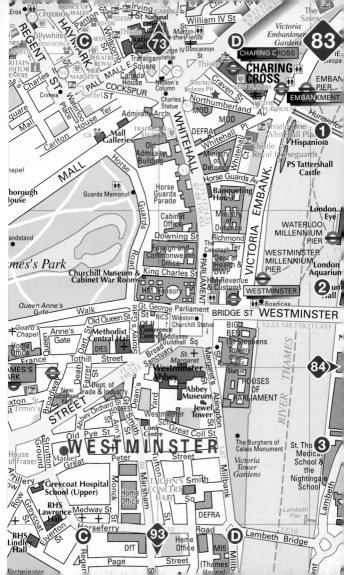

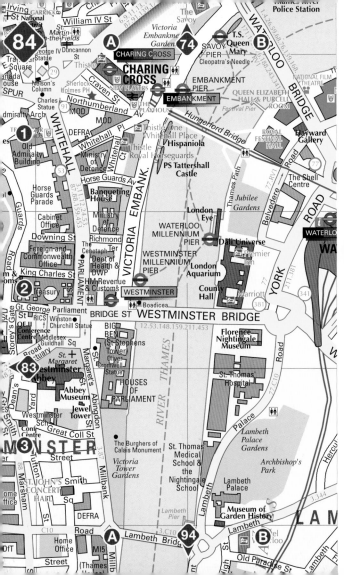

84

Irving St
National
Trust
William IV St
The
Savoy
Thames River
Police Station
Victoria
Embankment
Garden
St
Martin-the-Fields
George IV
Duncannon St
Statue
A CHARING CROSS
74 SAVOY PIER
T.S. Queen Mary **B**
Cleopatra's Needle

CHARING CROSS

NEW PLAYERS

Trafalgar
Square
anada
ouse
Nelson's
Column
Sherlocke
Holmes PH
Northumberland
Av

EMBANKMENT
PIER

SPUR
Charles I
Statue
dmiralty Arch
Craven St
THE
PLAYHOUSE

EMBANKMENT

QUEEN ELIZABETH
HALL & PURCELL
ROOM

NATIONAL FILM
THEATRE

1 Old
Admiralty
Building
MOD
MOD
DEFRA
Whitehall Pl
Hungerford Bridge
Thistle One
Whitehall Place
Thistle
Royal Horseguards
Hispaniola

ROYAL
FESTIVAL
HALL

Festival Pier

Hayward
Gallery

WHITEHALL
Ministry
of
Defence
Horse Guards Av
**PS Tattershall
Castle**

Thames Path

77
The Shell
Centre

Horse
Guards
Parade
Banqueting
House
Ministry
of
Defence
Richmond
Ter
**London
Eye**
Jubilee
Gardens

Cabinet
Office
The Cenotaph
Dept of
Health &
DWP
WATERLOO
MILLENNIUM
PIER
Dali Universe

Downing St
Foreign and
Commonwealth
Office
HM Revenue
& Customs
WESTMINSTER
MILLENNIUM
PIER
Premier
Inn

WATERLOO

WA

& King Charles
oms
2 Treasury
WESTMINSTER
Boadicea
**London
Aquarium**
County
Hall
Marriott

Gt. George
St
RICS
Parliament
Winston
Churchill Statue
BRIDGE ST WESTMINSTER BRIDGE

YORK ROAD

Storey's Gate
St
QEII
Conference
Centre
Broad
tuary
Middlesex
Guildhall
Sq
BIG
BEN
St Stephens
Tower
Oliver
Cromwell
Statue
Florence
Nightingale
Museum

83 estminster
Abbey
St.
Margaret
Margaret's
**HOUSES
OF
PARLIAMENT**
St. Thomas'
Hospital

Dean's Yd
Abbey
Museum
Jewel
Tower
Abingdon St

Westminster
Sch
M ST R
Great Coll St
3
Street
The Burghers of
Calais Monument
St. Thomas
Medical
School &
the
Nightingale
School
Lambeth
Palace
Gardens

Archbishop's
Park

ST JOHN'S
CONCERT
HALL
 office
Tufton
Smith
Sq
Victoria
Tower
Gardens
Lambeth
Palace

DEFRA
Marsham

Home
Office
DfT
ST JOHN'S
MI5
(Thames
Museum of
Garden History

A Lambeth Bridge
94
B

Old Paradise St

RIVER THAMES

Lambeth Pier

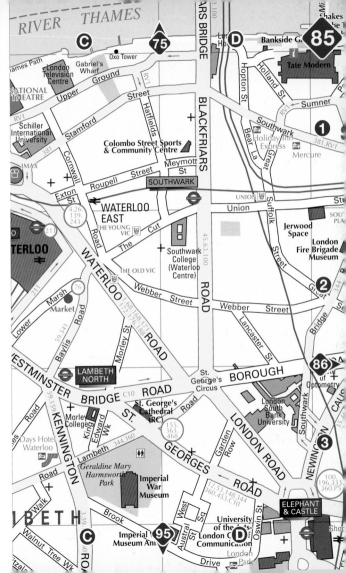

RIVER THAMES

C

75

BLACKFRIARS BRIDGE

D

85

Bankside G.

Shakes
the
Ex

Tate Modern

Thames Path
London
Television
Centre
Gabriel's
Wharf

Oxo Tower

NATIONAL
THEATRE

Upper   Ground

Street

RV1

Hopton St

Holland St

Sumner

Schiller
International
University

Stamford

Hatfields

381

Colombo Street Sports
& Community Centre

Cornwall

Roupell   Street

Meymott
St

SOUTHWARK

BLACKFRIARS   ROAD

Bear La

Great

Southwark

Holiday Inn
Express

Mercure

1

381.RV1

IMAX

Exton
St

4.26,
139,
243

WATERLOO
EAST

THE YOUNG
VIC

The

Cut

UNION

Union

Suffolk

SOU
PLA

ERLOO

211

211

Southwark
College
(Waterloo
Centre)

45.63.100

Street

Jerwood
Space

London
Fire Brigade
Museum

THE OLD VIC

Webber   Street

2

Great

Bridge

Marsh
Market

76

Waterloo   Road

Webber   Street

Lancaster St

59.341

168,168,171
172,176,188

Baylis   Road

Morley St

LAMBETH
NORTH

BOROUGH

86

of
Optometry

WESTMINSTER

59,159

C10

BRIDGE   ROAD

KENNINGTON

Morley
College

Edward
Wk

King

ST.

St. George's
Circus

GEORGE'S   ROAD

St. George's
Cathedral
(RC)

LONDON   ROAD

London
South
Bank
University

Southwark

NEWINGTON   CAUS

3

Days Hotel
Waterloo

Road

Lambeth   344.360

155,
363,
468

GEORGES   ROAD

Garden
Row

Road

Geraldine Mary
Harmsworth
Park

Imperial
War
Museum

12.51.148.344
360.453.C10

ELEPHANT
& CASTLE

Oswin St

Sho

I B E T H

3.59

Brook   Road

Walnut Tree Wk

C

Imperial
Museum Ann

95

West
St

St

Austral St

University
of the
London C
Communication

D

London
Park

Drive

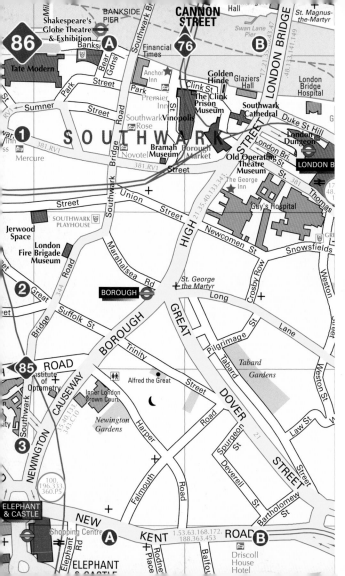

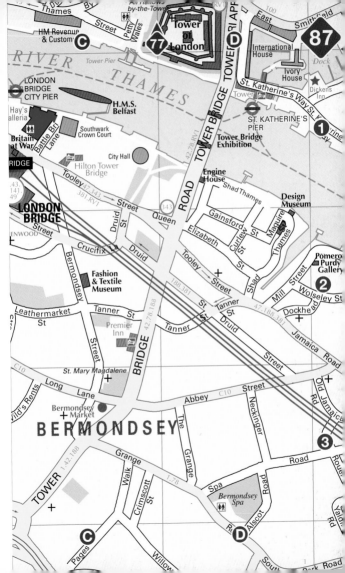

Thames Street

HM Revenue & Customs **C**

Petty Wales

77

Tower of London

All Hallows by-the-Tower

East Smithfield

D

International House

Ivory House

Dock

St. Katherine's Way SL.K

Tower

Dickens Inn

RIVER THAMES

Tower Pier

LONDON BRIDGE CITY PIER

H.M.S. Belfast

ST. KATHERINE'S PIER

1

rine

Hay's alleria

Battle Br Lane

Southwark Crown Court

Tower Bridge Exhibition

Britain at War

RIDGE

City Hall

Hilton Tower Bridge

Engine House

Shad Thames

Design Museum

.43.141 49'

Tooley 47.343 381.RV1 Street

343

Queen

Gainsford

St

Curlew St

Maguire

Thames

LONDON BRIDGE

Druid St

Elizabeth

St

Pomero Purdy Gallery

2

ENWOOD Street

Crucifix La

Druid

Tooley St

Street

Shad

Mill Street

Wolseley St

Dockhe

Bermondsey

Fashion & Textile Museum

Tanner St

188.381

St

Tanner St

47.188.381

Jamaica Road

Leathermarket St

Premier Inn

Tanner

BRIDGE ST

Druid Street

Old Jamaica

ild's Rents

St. Mary Magdalene

Long Lane

Abbey C10 Street

Neckinger

Rd

3

BERMONDSEY

Bermondsey Market

The Grange

Road

Roue

TOWER 1.42.188

Grange Walk

Crimscott St

1.78

Spa

Alscot Rd

Bermondsey Spa

Valor Rd

C

Pages

Willow

D

South

Park Road

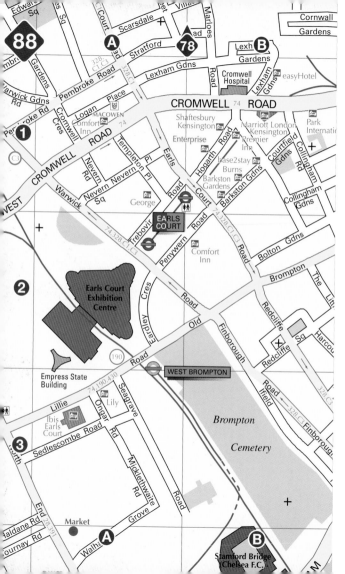

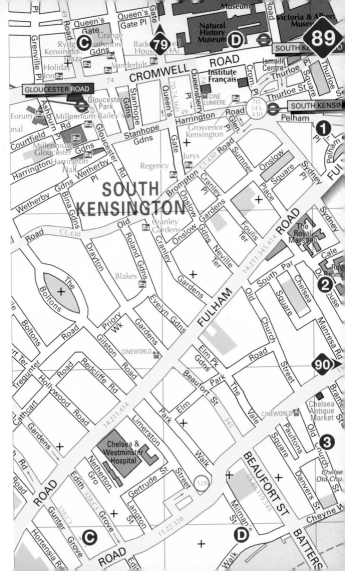

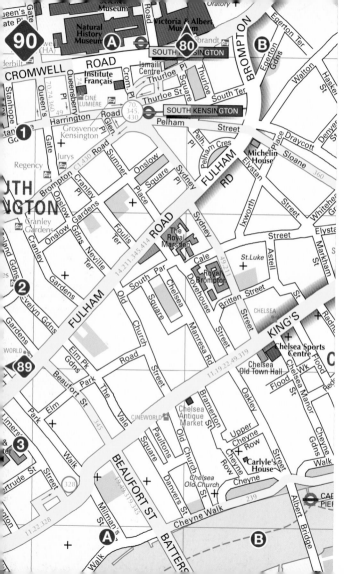

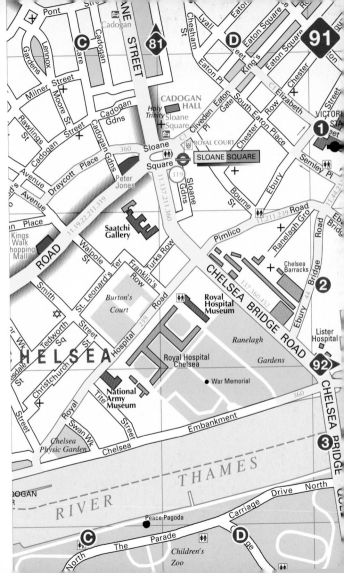

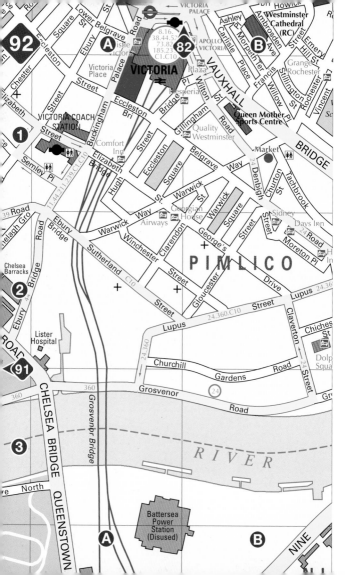

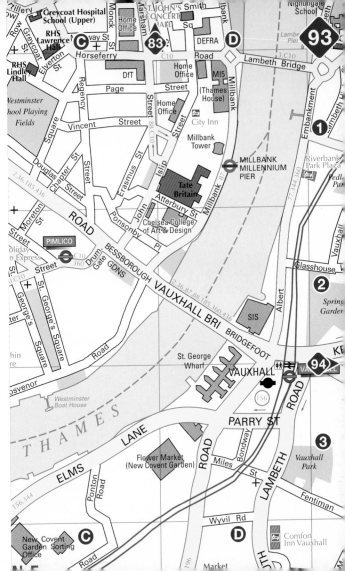

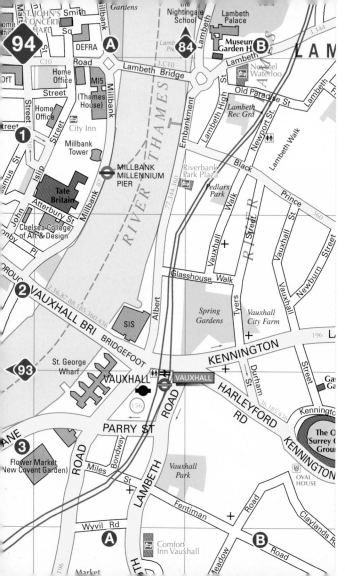

How to use this index

This index combines entries for street names, place names and other important features. Place names are shown in capital letters e.g. MAYFAIR. Street names are shown in black e.g. Oxford Street.

Other places are shown in blue and are distinguished by the following symbols:

●	Place of interest
🏥	Hospital
⇌	Railway station
↻	London Overground station
⊖	London Underground station
DLR	Docklands Light Railway station
Riv	Pedestrian ferry landing stage
⌂	Major hotel
♜	Theatre or concert hall
♛	Cinema
£	Important shop, shopping centre or market
ℹ	Information centre for visitors

All entries are followed by the page number and map square where the name can be found.

Abbreviations used in this index

App	Approach	La	Lane
Ave	Avenue	Mkt	Market
Bdy	Broadway	Ms	Mews
Bldgs	Buildings	N	North
Bri	Bridge	Par	Parade
Ch	Church	Pk	Park
Chyd	Churchyard	Pl	Place
Circ	Circus	Rd	Road
Clo	Close	Ri	Rise
Cres	Crescent	S	South
Ct	Court	Sq	Square
Dr	Drive	St	Street
E.	East	St.	Saint
Embk	Embankment	Ter	Terrace
Flds	Fields	Twr	Tower
Gdn	Garden	Vill	Villas
Gdns	Gardens	W	West
Grd	Ground	Wd	Wood
Grn	Green	Wf	Wharf
Gro	Grove	Wk	Walk
Ho	House	Yd	Yard

97

99

103